THE CREATIVE
COMPASS

THE CREATIVE COMPASS

WRITING YOUR WAY FROM INSPIRATION TO PUBLICATION

DAN MILLMAN
AND
SIERRA PRASADA

H J Kramer

published in a joint venture with

New World Library
Novato, California

An H J Kramer book

published in a joint venture with

New World Library

Editorial office:
H J Kramer Inc.
PO Box 1082
Tiburon, California 94920

Administrative office:
New World Library
14 Pamaron Way
Novato, California 94949

Text design by Tona Pearce Myers

Library of Congress Cataloging-in-Publication Data is available.

First printing, October 2013
ISBN 978-1-932073-65-2

Printed in Canada on 100% postconsumer-waste recycled paper

10   9   8   7   6   5   4   3   2   1

As HALLEY'S COMET streaked across the night sky, Samuel Langhorne Clemens was born. Years later, after making a reputation for himself under the pen name Mark Twain, he declared with characteristic audacity that he would die only after he'd seen Halley's comet once more. On April 20, 1910 — seventy-four years after his birth — that comet reappeared. The very next day, Sam died.

Soon after, a journalist visited Hannibal, Missouri, and spoke to some of the author's old cronies, one of whom remarked, "Heck, we all knew the same stories as Sam did — we just never bothered to write 'em down."

We wrote this book for all those
who bother to write 'em down.
And for Joy, who connects the dots between us.

CONTENTS

DRAFT

DEVELOP

REFINE

SHARE

FOREWORD

THE BOOK BEFORE YOU, written by Dan Millman and his daughter Sierra Prasada, a published author in her own right, shows how to develop and refine the way you think about and approach your writing, and outlines how to accomplish the goals you have set for yourself. Through a series of questions and well-developed answers, father and daughter look separately and together at what they have discovered about their own writing and the writing of others.

Much of what they suggest about how to become a better writer centers on determined, committed, and organized effort. They remind us that the quality of our daily life and action is reflected in the writing we produce.

In *The Creative Compass*, Dan and Sierra offer advice on all aspects of the writing life. From the first glimmerings of an idea to the completion of a polished piece; from dreams of seeing your work in print to the reality of being published; from feeling lost to finding a way — it's all here.

Thoughtful, thorough, and practical in its application, this is an important work on the creative process, and on the craft, business, and magic of writing.

Read it through. Decide for yourself. You won't regret it.

— TERRY BROOKS

PROLOGUE:
YOUR STORY, OUR STORY

The only end of writing is
to enable the reader better to enjoy life,
or better to endure it.

— SAMUEL JOHNSON

YOU MAY NOT HAVE REALIZED IT YET, but you're a storyteller. Whether you write fiction or nonfiction, whether you make films, speak to large crowds, care for children, or work at an office — every day, you swap stories with family, friends, colleagues, and even strangers. Few of us would ever think to call ourselves storytellers. Yet we all take a sweet, deep pleasure in telling *good* stories, some of them true. Like this one:

Not so very long ago, a young girl showed her father something she'd written, a part of herself, upon which he lavished the same attention that he gave to his own published work. Even as she herself began to publish in newspapers, magazines, and books, she continued to show her writing to him. Soon she began to critique his work in turn, and mentorship evolved into a collaboration that balanced his experience and perspective with her energy and ingenuity. That collaboration led to spirited conversation about what it means to make one's own way as a storyteller and writer, and to a partnership, as father and daughter became coauthors.

In this book we share with you an adaptable approach to any creative project, grounded in a cycle of five universal stages: Dream, Draft, Develop, Refine, and Share. No matter your level of experience, you'll find something about this cycle's basic structure familiar. We're all intuitively aware that works of invention begin with an idea and emerge from ritual and labor. Yet it remains mysterious how a finished book, for instance, could have started as a draft, or a full-length symphony from a simple melodic phrase. As members of an audience, we usually reach for words like *talented*, *genius*, or *brilliant*, even *miraculous*, to describe transformations that we can't witness and don't understand. But the key to such transformation lies in a dynamic attitude toward dreaming, a layered approach to drafting, and, most of all, in distinguishing the fourth stage, Refine, from the third, which revolves around what we call development.

The Develop stage is the middle act in a cycle that repeats with each project and that you may return to more than once before you complete each project, like a wheel within a wheel. Development is where the magic happens and, because we're not magicians, we have no qualms about sharing the secrets of our trade with you. It's your trade as well, after all.

You'll learn how to conceive, begin, and stick with exciting new projects.

As you read on, you'll learn how to conceive, begin, and stick with exciting new projects. You'll find your way in conversation with yourself, fellow writers, early readers, characters, and the world at large. It won't be one so-called best way, and most likely not the way you first seized upon, but rather the way that you determine, over time and trial, best serves you and your creative work.

As you read on, you'll dream up new ways to develop both your work and yourself. You'll learn how to surmount obstacles, on and off the page, by drawing upon what we call Master Metaphors, experiences that can make you believe in your own untapped potential.

Woodrow Wilson once said, "I use not only all the brains I have, but all I can borrow." After his example, we supplement our own experience with sage advice from Chinua Achebe, Isaac Asimov, Terry Brooks, Junot Díaz, Jennifer Egan, Albert Einstein, E. M. Forster, Marilyn French, Gabriel García Márquez, Elizabeth Gilbert, Kazuo Ishiguro, Ha Jin, Carl Jung, Mary Karr, Rudyard Kipling, Madeleine L'Engle, Laila Lalami, John le Carré, Spike Lee, David Morrell, Toni Morrison, Sylvia Plath, Constantin Stanislavski, John Steinbeck, Henry David Thoreau, Mary Heaton Vorse, and many more writers.

It's no accident that the experiences of so many writers and thinkers resonate with the model presented here — we've identified and described the five stages rather than inventing them. These stages also captured our own process in writing this book. The five stages apply equally to narrative and expository writing. In writing about story craft, we articulate and explore a set of foundational values with wide relevance, including purpose, clarity, coherence, brevity, accuracy, sensitivity, and ethics.

The five stages apply equally to narrative and expository writing.

Whatever wisdom we ourselves have to share comes directly from what Socrates might have called the "examined life" — in select chapters, we include personal narratives, showing how our approaches have evolved and continue to do so. Over the years, we've written novels, nonfiction books, works of memoir, and articles for print and the web. We've edited manuscripts in many genres and taught writing seminars and classes. And we've also achieved mastery in seemingly unrelated fields — one of us is a former world champion gymnast, and the other is proficient in Arabic — which provides us each with our own Master Metaphor, as well as insights into the power of process, the value of effort over time, and the essential interconnectedness of creative disciplines.

We draw upon our own experience to offer practical, concrete advice on writing, editing, and twenty-first-century publishing. You can benefit from this counsel regardless of whether you approach our shared practice as a beloved pastime or seek a fulfilling career.

In working together on this book, we honored the part of writing that is inherently collaborative. We drafted chapters individually. Then we edited each other's work to create a single voice, one that invokes that internal voice we've come to value whenever we seek guidance or encouragement. In the pages of this book, you'll hear that voice calling you to write your own way from inspiration to publication. We wish you good journeys.

ABOUT THIS BOOK

THE CREATIVE COMPASS guides your progress through a cycle of five universal stages as you advance toward your creative goals. Awareness of these stages equips you to navigate challenges with greater ease and to take advantage of opportunities, in writing and life, that you may not have recognized before.

At the Dream stage, a *sticky* idea calls you on a quest, and you set out to slay your own dragons.

At the Draft stage, you produce those early layers of writing that form your first draft.

At the Develop stage, a demanding middle act, you shape, cut, and rewrite draft after draft until your sentences and paragraphs anchor a coherent series of resonant ideas.

At the Refine stage, you seek comments from readers and editors as you distill your text down to an essence in which every word counts.

At the Share stage, you choose the most appropriate mode of publication, depending on your aims and the readiness of your manuscript.

For your convenience, this book has a linear structure, yet moving from one stage to the next may also mean doubling back and revisiting earlier stages as necessary. Each stage further re-volves around one objective that defines a pivotal task:

Dream: Define Your Story
Draft: Tell Your Story
Develop: Follow the Golden Thread
Refine: Choose the Right Words
Share: Move Your Readers

Would you like to become more inspired and disciplined? Are you seeking your true voice on the page? Do you want to know how to sharpen your instincts and acquire more meaning-ful experience? Read on.

YOUR QUESTIONS,
OUR ANSWERS

YOU CAN BEST UNDERSTAND the five stages by reading this book in its entirety. But we're presenting this index up front and in an FAQ format so you may jump directly to the chapters (listed below each question) that address your most pressing concerns. After you complete the book, you can also revisit this index to remind yourself that many others share your questions, hopes, and goals.

I want to write, but I can't seem to find the time or space. How can I become more inspired, motivated, and disciplined?

I journal often. Will it help my writing?

Writing in school made me anxious, so I wrote as little as possible. How can I possibly become a writer?

What can I do to find my voice on the page?

I'm feeling blocked. What should I do?

How do I know if I'm talented? If I'm not, should I bother trying?

I've read other books on writing, but I don't feel that my writing has changed. What else can I do?

I find outlining difficult. What else can I do to help prepare me to write?

I've studied books on craft, but my first drafts lack clear conflict, my characters seem shallow, and my language feels flat. What am I doing wrong?

Why does my writing seem so different from published books?

I want to write a popular book like The Hunger Games. *How can I learn to do that?*

When should I seek feedback and from whom?

How can I possibly make all the cuts my first readers have recommended? Aren't I mutilating my story?

How will I know when I'm done writing?

Dan: My Final Draft (page 205)

Agents repeatedly rejected my manuscript. Should I rewrite or move on?

Handling Rejection (page 220)

Should I submit to a publisher or self-publish?

Self-Publishing Pros and Cons (page 229)
The Nine-Sale Gauntlet (page 224)

Since I have no interest in publishing, my family says my writing is a waste of time. Are they right?

Get to Know Thyself (page 31)
Your Master Metaphor (page 124)
Dan: Reflections on the Writing Life (page 241)

Everyone publishes every *day. Aren't we all authors now?*

Sierra: Sharing on the Web (page 238)

My agent loves my third chapter; my editor hates it. Who's right?

Trust Your Gut (page 196)

I've finally had a book published. Can I quit my day job?

Marketing Your Book — and Yourself (page 233)
Epilogue: Your Writing Career (page 244)

Create your own method. Don't depend slavishly on mine.
Make up something that will work for you!
But keep breaking traditions, I beg you.

— CONSTANTIN STANISLAVSKI

INTRODUCTION

AS WE PREPARE TO EMBARK with you on this journey through the five stages, we share memories of our own beginning. We each felt a desire to tell stories before we developed any sense of how to do so. Like all writers, we needed to dream before we could draft. In these first two memoir chapters, and in the chapters that follow, we relate how insights derived from our life experiences have transformed our work as writers. Our trials may reflect your own, and we write so that you can share in the rewards of our labor. We're no longer beginners, yet we begin again and again, continuously propelled forward by a shared love of words and stories.

DAN: FINDING MY WAY

When you come to a fork in the road,
take it.

— YOGI BERRA

I WAS UPSIDE DOWN AGAIN. Not surprising, since I spent a good deal of my childhood that way, swinging like Tarzan from ropes or monkey bars, jumping from our roof wearing a make-shift parachute, or tumbling on a trampoline. Like my athletic dad, I felt more at home climbing a tree than sitting in a class-room. I enjoyed reading but showed no other signs of literary talent or inclination. Years would pass before the world would turn me right side up and I would find my way to writing.

In the meantime, I caught an occasional glimpse of the future: My ninth-grade English teacher, Ivan Smith (a.k.a. "Ivan the Terrible"), required us to write a short story each week — precisely two pages, immaculately typed, with the right-hand margin a nearly perfect vertical line, long before typewriters could do so automatically. Forced to edit every line to fit, I had to choose a shorter or longer word with the same meaning, which demanded an inventiveness I hadn't known I possessed. For the first time, I struggled to tell stories on paper.

(In an early example of fan fiction, most of my stories resembled plots from *The Twilight Zone*.)

Apart from that class, a creative peak in an otherwise undistinguished academic career, my preference for athletics over scholarship became a self-fulfilling prophecy. My first semester at UC Berkeley landed me on academic probation — a wake-up call that propelled me into survival mode. Applying an athlete's work habits to my studies for the first time, I earned high grades in my second semester and would maintain them for the rest of my college years. But my attitude toward the classroom hadn't truly changed — I found essay assignments and poetry analysis tedious and confusing. My earlier creative writing had faded into memory. Achievement in gymnastics dominated the foreground of my life as I won national and then world championship titles.

During my senior year at Berkeley, while volunteer coaching at the local YMCA and instructing at gymnastics camps and clinics, I discovered that I enjoyed teaching. Then, in my last few weeks of college, I made a pivotal connection between teaching and writing. As I turned in my final assigned paper, the thought struck me: *I can now write whatever I want — and maybe someday I'll write something worth reading.* I had no idea what that something might look like, but writing now represented a way of connecting with others.

As I turned in my final assigned paper, the thought struck me: *I can now write whatever I want.*

Soon after, a magazine advertisement caught my eye: Bennett Cerf, one of the founders of Random House, had created a correspondence course called The Famous Writers School, with the tagline "We're looking for people who like to write." Acting on impulse and faith, and committing most of my meager savings, I signed up. I threw myself into the course, drawing upon years of training in gymnastics and martial arts, with their emphasis on practice, endurance, and mastering the fundamentals. I mailed in each assignment and, a week later, received redpencil edits that helped me improve my work. Writing remained difficult, but it became an immersive pastime, generating a state of deep concentration that I'd experienced only in sport. Flow. The zone. Moments of silence, moments of truth.

Then life intervened: Marriage. The birth of my first child. The search for a career, or at least a day job. After finding a position as men's gymnastics coach at Stanford University, I sat down at my typewriter early each morning, stared at the blank page, and dreamed up instructive articles that I then submitted to *Gymnast* magazine. I later earned the title of contributor, my only compensation.

About a year later, while jogging around the Stanford campus on a hot summer's day, an idea came to me: *If the purpose of a fever is to heat up the body and kill unfriendly bacteria or viruses, could an exercise like running create an artificial fever to support the immune system?* Some research confirmed my hunch, so I wrote an article titled "Let's Catch Jogging Fever!" A few weeks later, a health magazine sent me a check for one hundred dollars. I had become a *professional* freelance writer.

Seven more years would pass before I earned another dime from my writing efforts.

After four years as a Stanford coach, I accepted a position on the faculty of Oberlin College in the Physical Education Department. Caught up once more in college life, I dreamed far more than I drafted. But, in hindsight, those years at Oberlin were some of the most important in my writing life. For three years, I taught and studied martial arts, practiced yoga and meditation, and traveled around the world on a grant from the college.

I eventually moved back to California, divorced, and later married again. All that life experience gave me something I wanted to share, but it hadn't yet taken any clear shape. Meanwhile, those articles I'd written for the gymnastics magazine had formed a thick stack on my desk. One afternoon, I glanced at it and thought, *That looks almost like a book manuscript.* Until that moment, it had never occurred to me that I might write an entire book.

Until that moment, it had never occurred to me that I might write an entire book.

Soon after, I began work on an untitled manuscript that would shape-shift many times over the next few years, out of the realm of physical training and into the arena of personal and spiritual growth.

I remember buying a fresh ream of paper as I walked to the UC Berkeley Women's Athletic Department to interview for a coaching position in the early spring of 1978. Four months later, by the time the athletic director finally offered me the job, I'd turned that ream into a draft of the book I titled *Way of the Peaceful Warrior* — beginning a decades-long roller coaster of a ride that continues today, more than thirty years and sixteen books later.

The winding path I've followed since childhood remains mysterious, more improvisational than strategic — for example, as improbable as it may seem, I made up my world championship trampoline routine in the moment and on the fly, one move at a time, up in the air while upside down.

It seems that our writing lives, no less than any athletic

feats, are stories of magical realism. We don't find a career in writing. It finds us once we make the choice to write, and then choose it again, day by day. The decades of work that followed my beginning brought a degree of wisdom appreciated only in retrospect, building on an amalgam of life experience, passion, labor, timing, and chance. Where it may end is anybody's guess and none of my business.

SIERRA: THE OTHER SIDE
OF ANXIETY

Our fears are a treasure house of self-knowledge
if we explore them.

— MARILYN FRENCH

I SAW FLOATING COLORS during the in-class essay, though I
don't remember Gatsby's green light among them. I can still
call to mind the tension of that sophomore-year English final in
1996. I'm seated in that chair, the pencil tight and slippery in my
hand as it scribbles in the blue examination book, but I'm also
standing behind my younger self. "It's just the beginning," I
want to say — I can see that now. Instead, I slip fully into that
moment. What I experienced then, I still want to understand:

The space of the high-ceilinged cafeteria seems to hunch
over me as I hunch over the table, intermittently aware of the
persistent scratching of other pencils. I've read Fitzgerald's
novel carefully, underlining whole paragraphs, filling up the
margins with notes. Nonetheless, about halfway through the
exam, I feel the bottom drop out from under me. I've rewritten
and rubbed out the same line so many times, it seems as though
the eraser will soon punch through the paper — and the specter
of all the remaining empty pages looms up at me and turns the

mundane world of final exams into a smeared kaleidoscope of flowing colors. Breath sweeping through me in gusts, I drop my pencil and leave the exam, sobbing.

I now look back on that day, from a distant mountaintop, as the pinnacle of my angst. Never again would anxiety overwhelm me so publicly, but overwhelm me it did, behind closed doors, despite the steps I took to ward it off — what I might, in those days, have called my process. I knew so little then and wanted so much. I guess that's what we mean when we talk about beginning.

Process then meant strict self-control. If I lost control, I believed, I might also lose the ability to write, to express what I wanted, to move forward in life. Armed against that possibility, in the days leading up to a writing session, I permitted myself to read no book apart from the one assigned, so as to thoroughly focus my mind. It was a painful sacrifice since I loved to read and would otherwise have taken refuge in books of my own choosing. I drew up elaborate outlines, studded with textual excerpts and notes that I'd transcribed. I spent up to an hour alone in my room — the only place I could write — agonizing over just the right title. I'm sure I didn't actually collapse in tears during every writing session, but it happened often enough that I remember it. I also remember what followed: I found my way into the piece. I drafted and revised it. And when I finished, relieved and exhilarated, the writing felt like mine, even though the forces that created it never did.

Too quickly, however, those good feelings on the other side of anxiety receded into the past, and the possibility of failure continued to claim my present and the future. Failure, at the time, meant nothing so trivial as a bad mark, but the total collapse of the self. It's no wonder that, by the time I graduated from high school, I wanted nothing more to do with writing essays.

Yet I also knew that writing mattered to me. I'd spent my leisure hours doing it. I edited the school newspaper and contributed to the literary magazine. I wrote news stories, features, film reviews, and astrology forecasts. A monologue I'd written in middle school had been published in two anthologies. In my senior year of high school, I took a playwriting class and wrote a one-act play that won the grand prize in a national contest. Is it any wonder that I majored in history, wanting to write about world events and people, and that I later went to journalism school?

I enrolled in graduate school with the fervent, mostly secret hope that deadlines would force me to deal with the enduring anxieties of the present. What changed me, however, was not journalism school, though its rewards were many, but writing *all the time*. The more pieces I wrote, the less each individual piece meant in itself. The more time I spent writing, the more comfortable I became with how much each individual piece did matter during that sacred period in which I worked on it. And over time, I revised my own process in the same way I would a story. All along, driven by my own stubborn desire to continually advance, I'd been learning how to revisit a piece with new eyes, as though from a different slant of self, so I could then rewrite what had seemed just right each previous time. With each new layer of work, new layers of words

> **What changed me, however, was not journalism school, though its rewards were many, but writing *all the time*.**

accumulated and extraneous layers fell away, like waves flowing in and out. I served the story, and process finally served me.

Not everything has changed: Behind one wall of my child-hood room lie cardboard and plastic boxes replete with old assignments. On my computer, I keep drafts of everything. Somewhere I still have that in-class essay that I eventually went back and finished writing.

I didn't know, for a long time, why I held on to them, papers that so little resemble what I enjoy reading or what I now want to write. Now, though, I think I understand. I keep those pages because they mean everything and nothing; because I loved them and hated them for exactly that reason; and because they were the beginning — but then again, so is every fresh page.

The human mind,
like the universe itself,
contains the seeds of many worlds.

— Loren Eiseley

INTRODUCTION

AS THE FIRST OF FIVE STAGES, Dream becomes the royal road to story. In the opening chapter, you'll learn why you need to permit yourself to dream so that you can generate an idea that matters to you over time — what we call your *stickiest* idea. You'll prepare yourself to draft by undertaking the primary objective of the Dream stage when you cultivate that idea and define your story. You'll bring your dreams down to earth by mentally sorting through and noting down elemental decisions about plot, character, story world, and setting.

As you get to "Know thyself," you'll become more capable of recognizing whether your creative process actually serves you and how to revise it if it doesn't. To that end, we recommend *dreaming in dialogue* — a simple conversational technique that reveals the perceptive questioner within yourself. This technique may help you identify your ideal reader and genre and connect with the appropriate audience for your work.

You can test the extent to which your essential story elements have come together by formulating a *What If* question. And, when you dream on deadline, you'll develop a new perspective on the constraints that make writing challenging but also enable you to turn your dreams into stories.

DREAM A LITTLE DREAM

I never came upon any of my discoveries
through the process of rational thinking.
Imagination is more important than knowledge.

— ALBERT EINSTEIN

WHEN WE DREAM, whether asleep or fully awake, we open ourselves to other worlds, and our dreams point us toward unexpected places, like a wardrobe that opens onto a magical land. And yet, we must dream with drafting in mind in order to make story possible.

In our daily lives, we tell stories of fact and fiction for a wider audience than ever before. So there's no task more essential to us than dreaming, or the cultivation of ideas, a pursuit long venerated by the sages. Socrates reminded young Athenians that "wisdom begins in wonder." Ralph Waldo Emerson might have been talking about dreaming in describing happiness as "a butterfly which, when pursued, is always beyond our grasp, but which, if you sit down quietly, may alight upon you."

In other words, wanting to tell good stories means first acknowledging that it's part of your work to make time for quiet sitting, for wondering at the world, for dreaming. But don't confuse the first stage with some nebulous trance or another purely receptive realm. The Dream stage calls for true discipline — not the knitted brow or other bodily tension that we falsely associate with discipline but a fusion of purpose with action. Worries will fill every available moment if allowed. Don't yield to them.

Do you long to create something of your own? Then make time to relax deeply into Dream. Set your mind loose to roam when you're stuck in traffic, for instance, or in the shower, cooking, or eating lunch at your desk. Let waves of ideas and images break over you. Every now and then, you'll connect with a sticky idea, the tightly coiled germ of a personally meaningful story poised to expand dramatically — not a blackbird, for instance, but Paul McCartney's "Blackbird"; not just any alien but Steven Spielberg's *E.T.*; not a room but Emma Donoghue's impregnable *Room*; and not the thirteenth-century Chinese emperor but Samuel Taylor Coleridge's *Kubla Khan*.

Do you long to create something of your own? Then make time to relax deeply into Dream.

In 1797, Coleridge woke from an opium-laced dream — itself influenced by some pleasure reading he'd done the night before — and rushed to his desk. He managed to set down "two to three hundred" lines of his famed epic poem with a "distinct recollection of the whole" before a visitor's interruption caused him to forget the remaining lines. In that visitor, we recognize the intrusion of critical judgment, which can undermine inspiration when it comes into play too early, snipping the buds of flowers merely because they have not yet bloomed.

Dreaming calls for patience and trust. It offers abundant rewards — but don't look to it for rules or guidelines. According to theater lore, on making his exit following one night's performance, Laurence Olivier strode directly into his dressing room and slammed the door. A friend knocked and said, "Larry, why are you so upset? That was one of the great performances of your career!"

"Yes," cried the actor, "but I don't know how I did it!"

Olivier didn't need to know how. Neither do you. You only need to set out in the direction determined by your imagination. Move forward with a whole heart and a smooth brow, trusting that a guide will come forth to meet you.

YOUR STICKIEST IDEA

Some ideas won't keep;
something must be done about them.

— ALFRED NORTH WHITEHEAD

SOME IDEAS ARE DIFFICULT TO REMEMBER; others are impossible to forget — in a word, they stick. Only your stickiest idea will inspire you to complete the journey you've begun.

Why? Plato wrote of Heraclitus's doctrine, "No man steps into the same river twice." Just so, identity itself fluctuates like a river. As time passes and you keep changing, once-dominant concerns become less important and then irrelevant. When tied to yesterday's preoccupations, even good ideas and plans fade away. But the idea that seizes your imagination and refuses to let go, the idea that matters to you on some deeper level — that sticky idea will hold your allegiance over time, and you'll draw energy from it.

Just take a look around you: You can find evidence for stickiness in every great work of literature, art, architecture, or innovation. The books on your shelf, the painting on your wall, the soup in that can — all emerged from nothing because they mattered to somebody, even when nobody else cared. And when you find your own sticky idea, it will cleave to you like a dedicated traveling companion: the Ambassador of Dream.

But where will this idea come from?

Ultimately, your stickiest idea will emerge from only one source: you. That is, your particular life, your own unique point of view, whatever moves you, not only on one particular day but on most days. Perhaps you've already snared such an idea with the net of your imagination? By all means, embrace it. But don't expect others to immediately recognize an idea's brilliance just because you find it enthralling. As computing pioneer Howard Aiken once said, "Don't worry about people stealing your ideas. If your ideas are any good, you'll have to ram them down people's throats." Your stickiest idea may creep in like a beggar long before it parades out as a king.

> **Your stickiest idea may creep in like a beggar long before it parades out as a king.**

If you're still looking for an idea to move you, you'll have to generate many before finding even one that truly sticks. But the verb *generate* doesn't quite convey the delicate interaction between receptivity and agency, inspiration and association, reverie and analysis.

The good news? As you dream toward drafting, you can work a kind of magic by engaging yourself in conversation, asking and answering questions about real or imagined worlds and the characters that populate them. (It's worth noting that during those blissful moments when we're fully absorbed in Dream, we still ask such questions of ourselves, but they flow by too quickly for us to consciously register them.) These questions, as well as the answers, will be specific to whatever event, individual, environment, or phenomenon intrigues you. So indulge your curiosity and, by all means, keep a list, even a notebook dedicated to the task. Berklee College of Music professor Pat Pattison refers to some familiar questions as the writer's "six best friends": Who? What? Where? When? Why? How? They're a good place to start.

You need to ask questions, in part, because your idea may not initially suggest anything more specific than its own stickiness. That idea, in its most nascent form, might be an image that strikes you: a girl wearing a white dress with one blue stripe, stalking away from you across a field. It might be the smell of something sweet burning in an otherwise empty room. Or a ripple of laughter resounding in an underground train station. As writers, we need to *cultivate* the stories within our sticky ideas. That's the work of Dream.

As writers, we need to *cultivate* the stories within our sticky ideas. That's the work of Dream.

If the present moment doesn't yield up any promising ideas, consider turning back to your personal history. Go through your computer files or the boxes in your attic, looking for images and articles you've saved. Find something, anything, that you labored to create and then held on to, whether a story or collage, a poem or pinhole camera. Remind yourself of the time you spent on it, and then ask yourself, *What made this stick?* The answer may surprise you, and it will tell you something true about yourself.

Novelist Ha Jin told the *Paris Review* that he might never have finished the first book he began in 1988 (and wouldn't actually complete for twelve more years), except that the idea stuck. "I just couldn't get the story out of my head," he said, "and I had to write to calm myself down." It's worth remembering that there's more than a measure of frustration in a sticky idea — it's a choice that can feel like a command.

That said, even the stickiest idea will slip away if you expect it to send you to your keyboard or glue you to your chair. No idea can force you to draft, but your stickiest idea will offer you a good reason to do so, even as it requires courage and stamina to carry forward. Sometimes we write only to develop courage and stamina. It's enough. To reach the moon, you'll need to build a rocket. Even your stickiest idea may need months or years to incubate. By sticking with it, you'll prove to yourself just how much that idea matters.

OBJECTIVE:
DEFINE YOUR STORY

I am willing to go anywhere, anywhere, anywhere —
so long as it's forward.

— DAVID LIVINGSTONE

ONCE YOU'VE CHANCED UPON a sticky idea, you may feel ready, even eager, to draft, but it's only time to embark on the objective of this essential preparatory stage: define your story.

How do you do so? By asking and answering key questions about plot, character, story world, setting, and theme. Such questions include:

❖ What will happen? What needs to happen first? What are the consequences?
❖ Who does what? To whom? Why?
❖ Where does the story take place? In other words, what is the story world? (Detroit? 1970s Moscow? Another planet?)
❖ What is the setting? Precisely where in the story world do pivotal and other events actually take place?
❖ How might the choice of story world and setting shape plot and character?

❖ What larger ideas or issues come into play through the story?

These questions will help you root out the story within your sticky idea if it hasn't yet revealed itself. You carry out this stage's objective when you distinguish between three elements: the original idea, which marks an unforgettable beginning; the story you envision, which becomes a kind of Platonic Ideal that you'll have to struggle to manifest on the page; and the act of dreaming itself, a determined campaign that takes creativity as its compass.

It's not enough to answer the above questions once. You'll need to rework them over time in order to make your story more effective. Pay attention to that word *effective*, because stories share a common purpose with expository writing and other works of art: to move us to believe, feel, think, and, in some instances, act. More concretely, when we write, we want to provoke and prolong our readers' desire to ask their own questions in order to resolve a mystery. For every story is a mystery story, and the mystery is: *What's going to happen next?* and *Why did it happen that way?*

Thankfully, any revisions you do in Dream will differ from those you do in later stages in a crucial way: you don't yet have a draft, so you won't have to do any redrafting. More than any of the stages that follow, Dream offers you the freedom to weigh the merits of competing alternatives as you make the global choices that constitute story definition and ˙design.

Dream offers you the freedom to weigh the merits of competing alternatives as you make global choices.

Whether you're content to think and rethink, or feel the need to take copious notes, the answers you ultimately draft from will influence every paragraph, sentence, and word of your story in the making. Be advised: if you begin drafting before thinking through essential story elements, then you'll likely need to make overarching changes down the line. The more text already in place whenever you make a change at the structural level (such as eliminating or taking on a major character or reversing a pivotal plot point), the more words you'll need to rewrite.

Imagine your story as a pool of water: if you throw a rock into that pool, it sends a ripple outward; the closer to the pool's center, the more ripples; the more ripples, the more revision. You'll never completely avoid development, the third stage, but devoting time and energy to Dream will help you limit its scope.

The questions around which this chapter revolves also define the key elements of story or narrative, which requires a central conflict enacted between two or more characters, set against one or more specific, meaningful locales. Conflict is the collision of desire, or will, with one or more obstacles. The protagonist wants something, but something else — usually another character, sometimes an aspect of her own character — blocks her from immediately achieving it. As John le Carré put it, "The cat sat on the mat is not a story. The cat sat on the other cat's mat is a story." The more motivated your characters are to achieve meaningful goals, and the higher the stakes of success and failure, the more effective the story.

For William Faulkner, story typically began with a character. "Once he stands up on his feet and begins to move," he said, "all I do is trot along behind him with a paper and pencil trying to keep up long enough to put down what he says and does." Even at the outset, you'll find it rewarding to approach your story from other angles by asking and answering questions on behalf of your characters: *Who am I? What do I want? What's in my way? What do I do to get what I want?* These questions and the answers you derive will remind you that each of your characters perceives and responds to shared events in a subtly or even radically different way. The more significant the character, the more their answers to the preceding questions will influence your plot.

Biographical stories begin with characters' births and end with their deaths, but your story, whether fact or fiction, will likely cover only a slice of lives more fully (though privately) imagined by you. At the Dream stage, go ahead and follow your characters into the past; consider their futures and ask yourself how they arrived there. Actors, also storytellers, know they can deliver more compelling performances by drawing upon earlier events that shaped their characters, even if these events are never explicitly revealed to the audience. You need to know more than you'll ever tell, and Dream's the time to undertake that exploration.

You're not yet drafting — consciously setting out to tell a story from beginning to end — but you may do a lot of writing, including general note taking, outlining, and free-associative mind mapping, as well as dreaming in dialogue and composing a What If question, techniques we address in upcoming chapters. Kazuo Ishiguro told Bill Bryson in an interview that he needs about two years to plan a story: "Every time I've got another novel to write I just can't believe that I ever managed to write one before," he said. "I do

> **You're not yet drafting — consciously setting out to tell a story from beginning to end — but you may do a lot of writing.**

desperate things. I make notes. . . . I'm not the kind of writer who can put a sheet of paper into a typewriter and improvise. I have to know more or less the whole structure of the book beforehand."

That's Ishiguro's process — only by experimenting can you determine how familiar you need to be with your story before you're truly prepared to draft. Regardless, the advance work you do here in Dream will double as ballast to ground and support your story, in the same way that objects uncovered at a dig or crime scene help archaeologists and forensic scientists solve their own mysteries. Professional investigators create stories about what happened in the distant or recent past, altering their narratives as necessary with each new relic that comes to light. Similarly, when you dream and plan, you're anchoring your story in comparable artifacts — images, fragments of dialogue, character biographies, notes on chronology and plot — and their weight will keep you on course.

As you dream, contemplate the multiple forms your story may assume, and take from them a fundamental lesson: commit yourself to the foundational ideas that underpin your story and not the phrasing that initially conveys them. In the words of graffiti from the streets of London, "Things slowly curve out of sight until they are gone, afterwards only the curve remains." The words that first suggest scenes, description, or dialogue are often placeholders, enabling the curve, or story arc, they evoke to coalesce as spirit — and only later as substance.

When you define your story, you give yourself the opportunity to make that story fully your own before you have to concern yourself with expressing it in a way that others can fully understand and appreciate. We each dream in our own individual languages, and drafting will always be an act of translation.

GET TO KNOW THYSELF

I always wanted to be somebody.
Now I realize I should have been more specific.

— LILY TOMLIN

IN THE DREAM STAGE, you need to look within in order to determine what stories you want to tell and how you'll go about telling them. When it comes to how you tell stories, it's essential that you clearly distinguish between your method of working, what we call *process*, and your fundamental creative decisions about key elements of story and structure that are generally referred to as *craft*.

Process and craft each contribute to how we tell stories, but process makes craft possible. More concretely, craft will enable you to cultivate ideas, but only process can ensure that you actually do so. When you make discoveries about process at this stage — when, where, and how you dream best — you find ways to spend more productive time defining your story, and you give yourself a better chance to effectively articulate and bring together story world, setting, plot, character, and theme, the overall objective of craft.

Mastery of craft can only emerge through process over

time, but it originates in your earliest recognition that the ancient dictate "Know thyself" describes a continuous practice rather than a single task that you can ever complete. Don't confuse this practice of self-awareness with self-absorption or self-consciousness. When self-absorbed, you become so preoccupied with your own internal monologue that you have trouble registering contrary signals from your environment. When self-conscious, you question and critique yourself to a degree that may compromise your sense of purpose. But when self-aware, you quietly observe your own thoughts and actions, gradually distinguishing what's natural from what's habitual and preparing yourself to make more deliberate choices as you advance toward specific goals.

In *Zen in the Art of Archery*, Eugen Herrigel describes archery as "a spiritual exercise" and writes that "fundamentally the marksman aims at himself and may even succeed in hitting himself." As you become more self-aware, you aim to inhabit the center of your actions so that they become an extension of yourself.

In Dream, we encourage you to internalize a cycle that supports the five stages: self-reflection leads to experimentation, which yields up periodic discoveries, which in turn trigger new episodes of reflection and experimentation. The overall purpose? This cycle will help you move beyond what merely *feels* right to what delivers results.

Move beyond what merely *feels* right to what delivers results.

In this and other chapters, we've formulated questions to help you begin a conversation with yourself — one composed of action as well as words — that will ultimately transform both how and what you write.

The following questions aim to help you get to know how you dream now:

* ❖ When and where do you frequently find yourself dreaming?
* ❖ What are you doing at the same time? Are you listening to music? Reading? Watching something? Moving around?
* ❖ Do you prefer to dream alone? If not, who's nearby doing what?
* ❖ In what form do ideas appear? As words? Images? Sounds?
* ❖ What do you do with these ideas? Do you record them? If so, how?

The questions we pose throughout the book have no right answers, only those that work for you. We urge you to periodically try out different ways of working so that process becomes a means to liberation rather than a rigid commitment to habit. In other words, your ultimate goal should be to identify your current capabilities, along with the routines that enable them, and then to surpass both, continuously expanding those situations in which you can dream — and later, draft, develop, refine, and share. Ask yourself: *What do I do regularly now that once seemed impossible? What made it possible?*

When it comes to craft, greater self-awareness also makes us better storytellers. We can invent stories that strangers find true and moving because our dreams evoke widely shared desires and struggles. In looking within, we also gain access to the same inner conflict that generates effective drama — whether it's cowardice we're battling (*The Neverending Story*) or the need for love (*Brokeback Mountain*). "We make out of the quarrel with others, rhetoric, but of the quarrel with ourselves, poetry," wrote William Butler Yeats, pointing to an essential human complexity and a persistent tension that underlie all masterpieces. As Yeats put it, "We sing amid our uncertainty."

When it comes to the work itself, however, uncertainty may also overwhelm you, forcing a self-preoccupation that blocks you from intuiting or inhabiting other lives and other worlds. In moments of crisis, the dark times when transcendence seems impossible and oblivion desirable, we urge you to take up or begin a journal. While self-reflection leaves no record and offers only a window through which to observe yourself, journaling enables you to step through that window. It doesn't matter what you write in, with what implement, or how you format the text. Journaling at its most purposeful means committing this conversation with yourself to paper so you can both write and read yourself. It means devising questions about your own process, answering them in writing, and rewriting them over time as an intermediary step toward revising your own choices and actions. One might even say that a journal can channel the deluge of your life's events into a more manageable and meaningful story form.

A journal can channel the deluge of your life's events into a more manageable and meaningful story form.

In addition, journaling can provide an outlet for unbounded self-expression and a stage for creativity. In Bernardo Bertolucci's film *Stealing Beauty*, the nineteen-year-old protagonist jots down short poems only to carefully tear them from her notebook and burn them. For her, at that time anyway, the act of writing means more than the words that go up in smoke and ash.

Alternatively, your journal becomes a bridge between dreaming and drafting when it acts as a writer's notebook, bristling with clippings, sketches, and ideas in the bas-relief of highlighter yellow or green. Sylvia Plath composed poems in her journals; George Orwell chronicled his adventures in gardening. Anne Frank made each entry of her diary epistolary, addressing her imagined best friend, Kitty: "I hope I will be able to confide everything to you, as I have never been able to confide in anyone, and I hope you will be a great source of comfort and support." To whom might you write?

However you choose to journal, we advise you to do so regularly — daily, if possible. Find a way that works for you. Write for five minutes. Write half a page. Give yourself a prompt, if it helps: Limit yourself to what happened today. Let an object in the room or a memory inspire sense-rich free association. Recall all you can of last night's dream.

Take the risk: free yourself to write without revising. Why does it matter so much? Because when you stare into the mirror of your own mind, also a filter of all your worldly experience, you discover in yourself a bottomless source of ideas and inspirations.

In the end, your journal serves as a living reminder that method produces matter, process leads to craft: it doesn't matter what you dream in any particular moment, only that you dream — and take notes — so you'll be ready to move forward in the direction that inevitably reveals itself as you come to know yourself better.

DREAMING IN DIALOGUE

Something I owe to the soil that grew —
More to the life that fed —
But most to Allah Who gave me two
Separate sides to my head.

— RUDYARD KIPLING

THE CONVERSATION WITH YOURSELF that you begin in Dream also doubles as a formal technique to kick-start a new work session, provide overall direction, and generate momentum. We've adapted an approach presented in David Morrell's book *The Successful Novelist*, and we've named it "dreaming in dialogue."

As an alternative to the traditional outline, Morrell proposes a written discussion between you (the "writer") and your alter ego, which assumes the role of a fellow writer or trusted friend. This conversation may run on for pages, depending on what you seek from it, the complexity of the idea you're presenting, or the complications you've run into. We've invented a few lines of a dialogue that might take place between you and your alter ego, after you've exchanged greetings:

Writer: And then my heroine will flee her uncle's house with his magic armor. After that I need her to reunite with the lover she's rejected.

Alter Ego: *Why did she reject him?*

Writer: Because he seduced her sister.

Alter Ego: *He actually did it, or your heroine just believes he did?*

Writer: Well, I hadn't considered the possibility that her sister might be lying — and that would make her so much more complex, but...

The gentle back-and-forth of the dialogue encourages a relaxed, discursive reflection — one that takes its intuitive order from the natural flow of ideas — and it will record ensuing discoveries. An outline, in contrast, requires from the start the same decisive organization it strives to represent.

The dialogue will guide you onto a clear if necessarily meandering path into the work.

Dreaming in dialogue is flexible enough to serve the needs of both top-down writers, who prefer to structure and then write, and their bottom-up counterparts, who generally write first and structure later. Regardless, the dialogue will guide you onto a clear if necessarily meandering path into the work, encouraging you to slip into a new project via a side door when you don't feel up to storming the ramparts on the heels of a declamatory battle cry.

Morrell credits a television interview with novelist Harold Robbins for inspiring this technique. Robbins confided that he began each writing day with an imagined conversation between himself and his typewriter, which addressed him in a woman's voice. As Robbins's approach suggests, you can alternatively converse with another part of yourself or project a supportive voice onto something or someone else. Robbins preferred to dialogue with an inanimate object that directly enabled his writing, something decidedly separate from himself, even to the point of embodying a different gender. Don't hesitate to experiment: unless one approach immediately feels natural, try each one in turn, and then develop one that works for you.

Through your artistic pursuits, you get to know the most creative and adaptable parts of yourself. When you dream in dialogue, you give these parts of yourself a voice that differs from your own and may be able to express insights that you hadn't realized you possessed. You've heard this voice before whenever you answered the question, *If you knew the solution to the problem, what would it be?* In addition, dreaming in dialogue counterbalances confused or negative thinking by redirecting the energy invested in that thinking toward the work itself — a strategy you can also bring to your wider life.

Beyond the creative realm, dreaming in dialogue can benefit anyone confronting a life challenge or a difficult decision. Only the subject of the dialogue changes. When we doubt or self-flagellate, whether about our writing or some more worldly challenge, we often forget that the same self we're berating for its incompetence has on other occasions also enjoyed well-earned confidence, arrived at sensible decisions, and generated great ideas.

Beyond the creative realm, dreaming in dialogue can benefit anyone confronting a life challenge or a difficult decision.

Building on this insight, you can assign opposing qualities to two different selves — or, to paraphrase Kipling, separate sides of your head — and then invite them to interact with each other. In this case, one side of your dialogue will represent the most uncertain, tentative, and concerned part of yourself. It asks questions that express doubts. The other side takes on the role of wise confidant, teacher, and mentor, deploying a range of tactics, such as gentle pressure or steadiness of mind, in accordance with what you want from it — because you're the one pulling the strings even if you're only half-aware of doing so. The teacher-mentor may lecture you, emphatic in its replies, or it may become an inner Socrates who answers questions with only more questions, coaxing you to devise your own answers and alter your process as necessary.

It may take some time to call up the side that incarnates your most hopeful moments and warmest relationships — the voice that tells you *everything will be all right* and overrules even your most panicked objections with an unshakable confidence that seems to hold a bright future in itself.

It's tempting to embrace the more positive side of your psyche, the *good* side, at the expense of the other — to see in one side only light, in the other only shadow — but the reality is more complex. As we come to understand ourselves, we recognize in our own doubt and self-censure an excess of the same qualities that underpin humility and caution. The power of dreaming in dialogue lies in the revelation that we actually need both sides of the self in order to live fully and to write well.

YOUR IDEAL READER

You have to put yourself
in the mind of the reader
you're trying to reach.

— SPIKE LEE

AS YOUR DREAM MOVES toward story, the time comes to ask yourself two questions in tandem: *What do I want to express?* and *To whom?* Your answer to the second question must shape your answer to the first because you dream not only of telling stories but of sharing them. Put another way, you'll tell better stories if you dream in dialogue with yourself *and* your ideal reader, who might sometimes take on the role of your alter ego.

John Steinbeck advised writers, "Forget your generalized audience. Pick out one person, real or imagined, and write to that one." When you write to connect with particular readers, you write for them: a fantasy with an eleven-year-old heroine for young adults, for instance, or a last-chance romance for senior citizens. Your work becomes a kind of letter to the specific, real or imagined and often remote individuals who stand in for your audience. As Junot Díaz put it in an interview with National Public Radio, "If...you're serious about participating in writing and in reading, you know that what you're really about is that you're trying to build a relationship with a reader...that you'll never meet and that you'll never see. And you want that relationship."

Your ideal reader might be your nephew playing video games in the next room while you define your story. Or the childhood friend who'll pick up the phone when you call with good news in the middle of the night. Or the understanding stranger who sat next to you in the train on what otherwise might have been the darkest night of your life. Regardless, you need to call to mind people who will motivate you to keep working on your story because they want to read it as soon as possible.

Direct your dreaming toward one archetypal reader or a like-minded group, and you'll define your story in a way that enables others to believe it and to feel what you feel. You don't have to know precisely what your story means in a larger sense — and underline this twice if you're writing memoir — but you do need to know what you want your story to mean to your readers and how you want it to affect them. Author and literary critic Cyril Connolly proposed that "it's better to write for yourself and have no public than to write for the public and have no self." But you don't have to choose — you can strive to please both yourself and your public by crafting stories that bring you and your reader together in mutual recognition of all that makes us human.

> **Direct your dreaming toward one archetypal reader, and you'll define your story in a way that enables others to believe it and to feel what you feel.**

That's not to say that any work will appeal to all readers. In the words of Carl Jung, "The shoe that fits one person pinches another; there is no recipe for living that suits all cases." Those who try to please everyone may not please anyone. The rare mega-bestseller, by definition, balloons beyond its target audience and genre. Fame, after the fact, doesn't mean the author had no initial audience in mind. J. K. Rowling, for instance, aimed her beloved Harry Potter series at young adults, not grown-up Muggles. Often, hitting the bestseller list takes authors and publishers by surprise.

All of which raises a related key question: What is your intended genre? Into which categories would you sort your favorite books, especially those you've enthusiastically recommended to others? Return to that conversation with yourself:

- ❖ Are you a dedicated mystery reader?
- ❖ Do you prefer literary novels? Thrillers? Self-help books?
- ❖ What's on your nightstand most nights?
- ❖ What kind of book might compel you to replace it with something quite different?

Remember that you are also someone else's ideal reader. Imagine, for a moment, pulling up a figurative chair to the table, resting your chin on your entwined hands, and listening to one of your favorite authors recount a tale of endurance and survival during World War II (*Unbroken*), or an inside look at a twentieth-century marketing genius (*Steve Jobs*), or a first-generation American's search for belonging (*The Namesake*), or a series of revelatory encounters between a psychotherapist and his troubled patients (*Love's Executioner*). Then, take a step back and ask yourself: *What makes me eager to know more? What moves me? What bores me?* Take notes so you can bring the understanding you gain back to your own story, because your readers want to be informed and entertained just as you do.

While your idea is still quickening within you, you can conceive your story as one you'd buy on sight and duck into the next café to read. This feeling alone will send you back to work. In an interview with the *Paris Review*, Toni Morrison said, "I never wrote a line until after I became an editor, and only then because I wanted to read something that I couldn't find. That was the first book I wrote." What better reason to devote yourself to a project than because you can hardly wait to read, watch, or listen to it, only it doesn't yet exist?

On the other side of such desire, however, waits the fear of dreaming up a story that's unique in the wrong way. Maybe it doesn't seem to fit neatly into an established genre. Maybe it takes an unusual vantage point on a person or relationship or event. Every new work appears to its creator in fantasies as potentially revolutionary in the best possible way, and in nightmares and dark moments as Dr. Frankenstein's monster, something that might not deserve life, that others may reject. Rest assured that fellow writers, even some of your favorite authors, have shared such concerns. If you get discouraged, go back to your imaginary readers and let them correct and console you as necessary.

If you get discouraged, go back to your imaginary readers and let them correct and console you as necessary.

These readers become even more important if you don't fall into your own target audience. For instance, middle-aged men have written fine young-adult novels with girl protagonists. In that case, you'll want to spend some quality time with these imaginary companions as you write, so treat them with respect — the more fully imagined they are, the better friends they'll be. You can tell them your story and, because you know them, you can carefully observe (read: anticipate) their reactions. You're gradually becoming accustomed to inhabiting other perspectives, even within yourself. And now, when all possibilities remain on the table because there's no manuscript yet — just the tantalizing idea of one — you can and should scan the faces of your listeners and ask yourself, *What are they telling me?*

WHAT IF...?

If you can't write your idea
on the back of my calling card,
you don't have a clear idea.

— DAVID BELASCO

BEFORE YOU DRAFT, you'll want to be able to clearly and succinctly answer that all-important question, whether posed by an agent or just a neighbor out mowing the lawn: *What's your story about?*

Fortunately, in the Dream stage, you can rely upon a proven technique to establish and strengthen your story's dramatic core — one that originated in a professional author's failure to clearly define his own story. After he'd already written a string of bestsellers, suspense writer John Saul received a five-word note along with the manuscript returned by his agent: "There is no book here." After rereading the manuscript, Saul agreed. He vowed never again to embark on a project until he could articulate the elements that sustain a dramatic narrative in one compelling sentence of no more than twenty-five words, a sentence he chose to begin with "What if...?"

Make Saul's lesson your own. Take the time to distill your story down to a one-sentence summary or What If question, a cousin of the elevator pitch and the film industry's log line.

Philosopher Bertrand Russell once quipped that "anything that can be put in a nutshell should be left there." But his colleagues dream of authoring elegant one-sentence proofs, and Saul's one-sentence question will enable you to define and refine the story concept that's emerged from your dream. A strong What If question will introduce the story's:

- ❖ Protagonist or central character
- ❖ Antagonist, or opposing force
- ❖ Essential conflict that pits the two against each other
- ❖ Genre and setting

Even a short story will contain more elements than can be captured in one sentence, and a long-form narrative will encompass additional background, subplots, supporting characters, complications, and revelations. But all these elements grow upward and outward from the seed of your sticky idea and the soil of your What If question.

The What If question lends itself most easily to story, whether fiction, memoir, or narrative nonfiction. It can also help define essays and nonfiction guidebooks by pointing toward the intended audience and indicating how the work will serve readers. We devised and fine-tuned a What If for this book: *What if we could demystify the writing process with five universal stages to help you reach your creative goals in writing and life?*

For most nonfiction, the title and subtitle together play a complementary role to that of the What If. Along with this book's title and subtitle, consider the following examples: *Guns, Germs, and Steel: The Fates of Human Societies*; *Up From History: The Life of Booker T. Washington*; *Freakonomics: A Rogue Economist Explores the Hidden Side of Everything*; and *The Audacity of Hope: Thoughts on Reclaiming the American Dream*. Peruse your own shelves or ereader titles page to see what other title and subtitle pairs have to tell you about each book's core idea.

If you find it challenging to come up with a compelling What If question, you may not yet have all the elements that make up a compelling story. So keep on revising your question until it captures the essence of the dream you want to share. Throughout the five stages, the What If brings your story back into focus while giving it room to evolve.

> **Throughout the five stages, the What If brings your story back into focus while giving it room to evolve.**

Applying the proverbial wisdom "I hear and I forget; I see and I remember; I do and I understand," we encourage you to compose What If questions for several of your favorite books. In doing so, you'll develop your own abilities as a storyteller because you're working directly on the most fundamental elements of story. First, here are some examples, each twenty-five or fewer words:

The Wizard of Oz: What if a tornado carried a young girl to a magical land threatened by a witch whom she must defeat in order to return home?

1984: What if love were declared a crime in a totalitarian future, forcing an ordinary man to become an outlaw in a daring quest for freedom?

The Lord of the Rings: What if a young hobbit and loyal

fellowship pursued a hopeless quest to destroy the Ring of Power desperately sought by an all-seeing wizard?

Matilda: What if a brilliant five-year-old, aided by a trusted mentor, found a way to triumph over her cruel parents and tyrannical teacher?

The Book Thief: What if Death narrated the story of a German girl who discovered, through her love of books, how to save herself and a runaway Jew?

Iran Awakening: What if a fervently patriotic attorney realized she would have to fight the revolution she'd championed if she hoped to save her life and her country?

What If questions remind us that literature expresses our hunger for the coherence and meaning that life doesn't necessarily provide. Moving between the real world and the dream, you may feel like Dorothy Gale when she murmurs, "Toto, I've a feeling we're not in Kansas anymore." In a world of imagination, is it any wonder that a one-sentence question can wield as much power as a pair of ruby slippers?

DREAMING ON DEADLINE

If the doctor told me I had only six minutes to live,
I'd type a little faster.

— ISAAC ASIMOV

BY ALL MEANS, enjoy the unique freedom granted by the Dream stage, but move forward to the next stage knowing that committing ideas to paper means working with constraints — and that you stand to benefit from them. We've chosen to highlight deadlines because they make progress through the five stages more likely. In this final chapter of Dream, we'll also explore the influence of related checks on *process* (our method of working) and *craft* (how we tell stories). These so-called limitations make writing frustrating, but they also force you to adapt and evolve when you make the most of them.

A deadline offers a valuable glimpse into your future: the suggestion and the prompt that you'll finish a project at a predetermined time, even a project you've only just begun. If you don't already dream on deadline, we urge you to try doing so. A drop-dead date, no matter how informal, will help ensure that you turn that dream into a draft and proceed from there. As we've previously said, a sticky idea won't fix you to your chair, but deadlines exist to do so.

Those of you who already write on deadline may have confronted a different challenge: *Where's the time to dream?* As we hope you've already discovered, however, you *can* dream on deadline: when you treat the Dream stage as a necessary prologue to the action and not a form of procrastination, you'll make up for any delay in beginning to draft by choosing the best, and not just the first, route to your goal.

As deadlines demonstrate in general, a constraint, at its base, obliges choice, and choice makes possible story, storytelling, and art — not to mention life itself. When it comes to the writer's craft, plot is a constraint that dictates what events can and cannot form part of a narrative. Any given character must claim a reasonable excuse for acting out of character. A story that unfolds in one setting or time period, for the most part, cannot simultaneously take place in an alternate setting or time period. These constraints, and others, not only point to the need for decisions; they help us make those decisions by offering direction.

When it comes to how you go about working, the impediments are more concrete: time, energy, willpower, and the need to balance commitments. Arnold Bennett's early twentieth-century self-help book, *How to Live on 24 Hours a Day*, isn't any less relevant today. As Bennett demonstrates, constraints may block one path, but they point toward others. What look like limitations when we resolve to do it one way only, become possibilities when we resolve to do it in whatever way works: "If my typical man wishes to live fully and completely," Bennett writes, "he must, in his mind, arrange a day within a day.

And this inner day, a Chinese box in a larger Chinese box, must begin at 6 P.M. and end at 10 A.M....During those sixteen hours he is free; he is not a wage-earner; he is not pre-occupied with monetary cares; he is just as good as a man with a private income. This must be his attitude. And his attitude is all important." It's a change in perspective, however, that's more practical than mere positive thinking: Who cares if the glass is half full or half empty when you can drink from either one?

> **What look like limitations when we resolve to do it one way only, become possibilities when we resolve to do it in whatever way works.**

Put most simply, deadlines and other curbs on our freedom remind us that, to use the expression of a former U.S. president, we're "deciders." We ask questions and we answer them in a singular way. Even before we draft, we make one decision after another, and all but the final layer of these decisions ultimately dissolves into the text like invisible ink. When we make new decisions about craft, we revise our work; when we make new decisions about process, we revise our lives.

All this raises another key question for you to ask yourself: *How purposefully do I respond to constraints?* The better you get to know the checks on your own decision making, the more adaptable you can become as you work with or around them — and the more importance you assign to those choices that will further constrain future choices. We benefit most from our constraints when they force us to become more practical and creative in the service of our ambitions.

On the level of each story or piece of writing, constraints will influence structure, topic, angle, and page or word count, as well as the number of possible revisions. Like the ancient gods of mythology, preconditions reward us when we honor them.

You're more likely to write a terrific eight-hundred-word story, for instance, if you conceive it as such and if you dream right up until you absolutely need to draft. Likewise, each genre challenges the writer to satisfy constraints in a novel way, to look on them as a challenge and not a choke hold. Dreaming on deadline means continuously learning how to do more with less in the service of a dream worthy of that name.

There are many six-hundred-page books, for instance — but only one *The Old Wives' Tale* or *Moby Dick*. As Herman Melville said, "To produce a mighty book, you must first choose a mighty theme." Journalist and author Gene Weingarten, while working as an editor, described how he directed writers to draw forth the mightiest theme from seemingly mundane assignments, blowing right by what seemed like built-in limitations. In the introduction to his collected features, *The Fiddler in the Subway*, Weingarten relates: "The writer would tell me what his story was going to be about, and then I would explain to him, patiently, why he was wrong. Your story, I would say, is going to be about the meaning of life." Weingarten then uses a series of questions to show how even news in brief about "the closing of a local amusement park" can invite readers to contemplate what it all means, transforming a few skim-worthy paragraphs into a potentially limitless portal for revelation.

Draw forth the mightiest theme from seemingly mundane assignments.

The time between the beginning of an assignment and its on-deadline conclusion often seems like a limitation, but we can reinterpret it as a portal for transforming both reader and writer. How? In our work, storytellers, like scientists, look for small phenomena that evoke much greater ones. Likewise, every writing assignment, no matter how small, puts you through a variation on the five stages, and the more such assignments, the more completed cycles. In contrast, long-form writers may take that much longer to cycle through all five stages just once.

Every writing assignment, no matter how small, puts you through a variation on the five stages.

Here, at the border of Dream and Draft, we have an opportunity to look ahead at the stages still to come. In observing your own progress from Dream through Share in microcosm on a daily, weekly, or monthly basis, you can more easily ask and answer insight-generating questions such as:

❖ What are my constraints, from most to least difficult?
❖ How do I deal with them now?
❖ How does my method of work already reflect the five stages?
❖ Is there a clear progression, or do different stages coincide?
❖ About how much time do I spend in each stage?
❖ Am I making effective use of the aids available to each stage — editors and readers, for instance — when it comes to Dream, Develop, and Refine?
❖ What's the practice to which I'm most attached? What would happen if I did something else instead?

Ultimately, as a deadline-driven writer who devotes constructive time to dreaming and planning, you'll draft better stories *and* develop a more effective process, because you'll realize that you can slow down even if the world won't do it for you. Even the chairs we relax into are themselves constraints in space.

Once you become fully aware of the curbs on your own writing, you'll find satisfaction and then joy in the agility with which you negotiate them. The flow of your ideas from the tap of inspiration will thicken. Before you finish any necessary research, you'll see entryways into a story or argument that would have remained obscure to an earlier outlook. You'll begin drafting at the appropriate time, while retaining the flexibility to flip or develop the piece if you discover some important new angle late in the project. Unexpected obstacles won't trip you up but instead will alert you to the possibility of capabilities you hadn't yet envisioned — a slightly altered reflection in the mirror, a different slant of self.

In other words: Clark Kent, don't forget that you're also Superman.

If you have built castles in the air,
your work need not be lost.
Now put foundations under them.

—— HENRY DAVID THOREAU

INTRODUCTION

By now, you've conceived and cultivated a sticky idea, but you reach the Draft stage only when you set out to re-create on the page the story of your dreams. Now it's time to tackle a fundamental act of creation, this stage's primary objective: tell your story from beginning to end.

In order to do so, you'll need to choose a storyteller. Don't strive for perfection in your early drafts, but do focus your efforts on sense and sensibility — as a start, you want your ideal reader to make sense of your story and to find it moving. Research need not slow your initial momentum if you resolve to begin with what you know and fill in what you don't as necessary.

You'll be more likely to move forward in drafting when you recognize it as an act of listening. And when you rediscover how to read writing books, you can apply the wisdom of more experienced peers to your own projects. In this section, we share insight on how to overcome the feelings of paralysis and self-doubt, and the fear of loneliness that come with drafting. We also encourage you to permit yourself to write badly in your early drafts — as all writers must — so that you will continue writing.

OBJECTIVE: TELL YOUR STORY

You imagine, before you start, there's a cathedral,
and the moment it starts on the page, it's a garden shed.
And then you just try to make it the best shed you can.

— SADIE JONES

ON THE MOMENTOUS DAY you begin to draft, you don't stop dreaming, but you refocus on this stage's objective when you begin telling your story on paper and for readers. The story you've defined through dreams, dialogues, and notes now comes with necessary constraints, those choices you've already made about what will (and won't) happen.

Like Adam and Eve, you've traded some of your freedom for knowledge. They can't return to the garden, but you can by staying open to inspiration and daring to experiment when you draft, even as you honor consistency. As the saying goes, "Stay hungry, stay foolish." Your draft is both material and mutable: if you find that you can't comfortably stay within the lines you've set, then you can move those lines.

In Draft, you continue to define your story; only this time, you put down sentences, and then paragraphs, that convey a detailed narrative, a logically continuous series of connected events with a clear beginning, middle, and ending. As you select events and string them together like pearls, bear in mind that in life one event happens after another, but in story one event drives another. Imagine as you draft that you're literally telling your story to that ideal reader seated just across from you.

Your What If question now becomes the spectacles through which you peer at and appraise each new choice; as you proceed, remember that what works on the page may justify amending your What If. Stay focused on your objective: nothing is more important to this stage than your doing whatever it takes to get a complete story down in words. Remind yourself whenever necessary that it's not yet time to brood over whether they're the best words — draft now, refine later.

Do whatever it takes to get a complete story down in words on the page.

If you're writing fiction, narrative nonfiction, or memoir, then your first draft needs to bring together a smaller story and a larger story. The smaller story introduces and follows specific characters and scenarios minted by your imagination. The larger story is primal, archetypal — it's the light that casts your smaller story into sharp relief, revealing the universal associations and deeper meanings underlying particular scenarios.

Broadly speaking, the larger story will itself adhere to one or some combination of two fundamental story types: a stranger comes to town or someone goes on a quest. Alternately, screenwriting guru Robert McKee defines story in terms of an initial incident that "upsets the balance of forces in the protagonist's life," compelling the quest for a desired object or goal to restore that balance. When a stranger comes to town, this initial incident originates outside the narrative and intrudes on the frame of reference, as when a spaceship brings a creature from another world or a horse bearing a cowboy with a secret rides out of the badlands. In contrast, when someone goes on a quest, the frame itself shifts, following the protagonist as she leaves home and strikes out for parts unknown.

Your chosen genre will, in turn, focus your imagination because each genre shapes the outcomes of stories that fall within it — and we can conceive genre in traditional terms (such as romantic comedy or suspense) or take into account fresh categories such as "dude with a problem" or "rites of passage," as presented in Blake Snyder's *Save the Cat!* screenwriting series. As film makes most clear, stories tend to conclude predictably: we know that the hero will likely vanquish the villain; that the lovers will usually be reunited, their quandary resolved; and that justice will most often prevail. Comedy requires a happy ending, tragedy a sorrowful ending, and noir a morally ambiguous ending. All of these genres, in addition to the two larger story types already mentioned, leave the *how* entirely up to the writer. In this *how*, we find the call to experiment that makes the draft such a radical document.

Your draft gathers energy from your willingness to strive for whatever best serves the story you're now building, in terms of action, description, flashbacks, dialogue, figurative language, or images pasted in between blocks of text — no matter how outlandish the material may at first seem. You can let your imagination loose to roam the territory you've staked out, knowing that you'll exercise more restraint in the Develop stage. In the meantime,

Don't let timidity or your own critical judgment disrupt the movie unspooling in your mind.

don't let timidity or your own critical judgment disrupt the movie unspooling in your mind. When you draft, you're half creator and half stenographer.

As you move deeper into your manuscript, a frame tale emerges, one in which you're the Scheherazade-like protagonist, and your draft itself acts as the beginning that makes an ending possible. Steady progress requires a push from start to finish that leaves little time for second-guessing or flaw finding. Choose continuity over closure: finish each writing session by composing the first sentence of a new paragraph or a new page. That way you'll sit down having already begun.

If you must, make it a habit to review or revise the last few paragraphs only — the equivalent of a runner stepping back in order to accelerate into the race. You're looking to outrun your own fears and doubts. And eventually, as your pages grow, it will come to you: you're the Ambassador of Dream now, the fleet-footed messenger god whose steps trace a legible path through a world of your own creation.

WHO IS YOUR STORYTELLER?

You cannot dream yourself into a character;
you must hammer and forge yourself one.

— JAMES ANTHONY FROUDE

THE FIRST FEW LINES of your draft must answer another fundamental question: *Who, on the page, will tell the tale?* If you haven't already done so, it's time to decide on a narrator and mode of narration: the first person (speaking as *I*), the second person (addressing *you*), or the third person (describing *he*, *she*, or *they*).

How much do these narrative choices matter to the substance of the story? Think about it this way: When a friend tells you something personal, you evaluate tone, intention, and believability based upon what you know of that person, a character from your own life. In the same way, your choice of narrator and mode of narration dramatically influence readers' emotional experience of your story. Once you perceive the narrator in your friend, it may be easier for you to recognize the character in your narrator, whether you opt for first-, second-, or third-person narration.

Conceiving of your narrator as a character — one who serves as an intermediary between other characters and your readers — will help you approach storytelling from a new angle and make more deliberate choices. To do so, however, you first need to understand the specific effects of each narrative mode on how readers relate to stories.

Your choice of narrator and mode of narration dramatically influence readers' emotional experience of your story.

In first-person fiction or memoir, readers observe the story world through one individual's eyes and can only see the narrator via her own descriptions of herself and her interactions with other characters. This narrator may or may not be the protagonist of the work — and these two alternatives produce substantially different effects. By making Nick Carraway the first-person narrator of *The Great Gatsby*, for instance, F. Scott Fitzgerald allows readers to closely interact with his title character even as the inner workings of Gatsby's mind remain inviolate, making possible various mysteries around which the plot revolves. If you're familiar with the novel, it's worth taking a moment to consider: How different would it be if Jay Gatsby narrated his own book? How would other stories change if their narrator or mode of narration changed?

In the second-person point of view (less frequent in all but songwriting and instructional books), the narrator addressing *you* takes on a more oblique presence, revealing aspects of himself only through his manner of speech. Second-person narration either directly addresses the reader or treats *you* as the work's protagonist. Mohsin Hamid cast his satiric novel *How to Get Filthy Rich in Rising Asia* entirely in the second person:

Look, unless you're writing one, a self-help book is an oxymoron. You read a self-help book so that someone who isn't yourself can help you, that someone being the author.... Some might even say it's true of religion books. But some others might say that those who say that should be pinned to the ground and bled dry with the slow slice of a blade across their throats.

Second-person narration often makes use of the imperative, that is, speaking in commands, as in the opening lines to Katherine Boo's nonfiction narrative *Behind the Beautiful Forevers*: "Let it keep, the moment when Officer Fish Lips met Abdul in the police station. Rewind, see Abdul running backward away from the station and the airport toward home. See the flames engulfing a disabled woman in a pink-flowered tunic shrink to nothing but a matchbook on the floor." In the first few pages of his novel *The Crimson Petal and the White*, Michel Faber draws upon the second person to teasingly relate the desire for an absorbing book and a willing prostitute, as the book itself taunts the reader: "Let's not be coy: you were hoping I would satisfy all the desires you're too shy to name, or at least show you a good time." Boo's, Hamid's, and Faber's narration serves to beckon readers into the story and then direct our focus elsewhere.

A story enacted strictly in the third person resembles a dinner party at which the guests can see everyone but the host — the narrator — who presides over the gathering all the same. "Some years ago there was in the city of York a society of magicians," opens Susanna Clarke's novel *Jonathan Strange & Mr*

Norrell. "They met upon the third Wednesday of every month and read each other long, dull papers upon the history of English magic."

Third-person narration comes in two flavors: Omniscient narrators, as the adjective suggests, know absolutely everything about your story and characters, usually including what those characters think or feel, but these narrators reveal little or nothing about themselves. Close third-person narrators, in contrast, limit themselves to the point of view of one character, or sometimes one character at a time; readers know only what that character knows at any given moment. Pat Barker's close third-person narrator in her novel *The Ghost Road* takes on the attitude of her protagonist, Billy Prior, even before he's introduced:

> In deck chairs all along the front the bald pink knees of Bradford businessmen nuzzled the sun. Billy Prior leant on the sea-wall. Ten or twelve feet below him a family was gathering its things together for the trek back to the boarding-house or railway station. A fat, middle-aged woman, swollen feet bulging over lace-up shoes, a man with a lobster-colored tonsure — my God, he'd be regretting it tomorrow — and a small child, a boy, being towelled dry by a young woman.

As this example shows, if you choose a close third-person narrator who takes the perspective of a particular character, then your narration needs to harmonize with, even mimic, the voice of that character as otherwise represented in dialogue.

It's worth briefly noting that because narrators tell the stories, their voices, more than that of any other character, establish each story's style and texture, both in terms of what's said and how it's said. We come to know the story world vicariously through the narrator's description and the sensations of characters. We physically experience words — consonants and vowels coming together and splitting apart — with our minds when we read, with our ears when we listen, and with our mouths when we speak. It's not yet time to focus on language, but you can benefit from approaching drafting as a sensual act.

When you write first-person fiction or memoir, your narration also carries the burden of depicting and delineating the point-of-view character represented by *I*. Bear in mind, readers know a lot less about your *I* than you do as the author — they won't even know the gender of your narrator until you tell them. Personal essayist Phillip Lopate points out that, for authors, the "*I* swarms with a lush, sticky past and an almost fatal specificity, whereas the reader encountering it for the first time in a new piece of writing sees only a slender telephone pole standing in the sentence trying to catch a few signals to send on." In other words, that *I* can transmit only those signals that your text itself — that is, your narration — makes possible.

> **Bear in mind, readers know a lot less about your *I* than you do as the author.**

This smaller truth of narration points to a larger one: when you read your own work, you first approach it as an extension of your own mind. You'll have to make a special effort to differentiate between all that you bring to a draft — such as the entirety of your personal history, when it comes to memoir — and the lesser degree of insight experienced by your readers, most of whom know nothing about you or your story beyond the words printed on the page. Here you discover a literary corollary to the fundamental mystery of human consciousness: the reality of your own mind so dominates that, on and off the page, you'll need to continually remind yourself that readers don't have access to the same thoughts and feelings that you do.

As an experiment, take up one of your own journal entries or a letter or email you've written, and imagine a stranger reading it one year or ten years or one hundred years into the future. Review it sentence by sentence and ask yourself:

❖ What does the reader learn from each sentence about my world and me?

❖ How much less might the reader understand as the distance between us (in time and geographic space) increases?

❖ What other slight additions to the text would allow the reader a more meaningful view?

The insight derived from such an exercise will make the gap between writer and reader more concrete — and help you narrow it. As Jay R. Gould said, "Writing is simply the writer and the reader on the opposite ends of a pencil; they should be as close together as that." On a practical level, acknowledging the extent to which your narrator's voice forms the envelope of the story will allow you greater distance from which you can later evaluate the effectiveness of your own storytelling and the coherence of your exposition.

As you begin drafting, you may need to experiment before you settle on the most appropriate narrator. It's never easy to speak in another's voice; even experienced writers sometimes run up against their own limitations when working with narration and must act to compensate for them. Australian author Markus Zusak initially thought the young German protagonist Liesel should narrate his novel *The Book Thief*, but then he realized it wouldn't work. As he told the website Mother Daughter Book Club: "I used Death as the narrator, because when I had Liesel writing the book she was the most Australian-sounding German girl in the history of writing." The final text unites first-person and close third-person narration. "The voice of Liesel definitely comes through . . . and you see things from her point of view," Zusak explains. He ultimately chose Death as the narrator because Death revealed himself as a character with a powerful objective: "I thought . . . 'It makes sense that [Death] is telling this story to prove to himself that humans can be beautiful and selfless as well.'"

This anecdote makes clear just how much three questions shape each story: *Who is telling the story? To whom? Why?*

Three questions shape each story: *Who is telling the story? To whom? Why?*

We can also apply these questions to our own lives. We're aware of ourselves as having *character* — in the sense of personal traits and values, and a unique way of viewing and interacting with the world. But it requires another step for us to recognize the character, and the narrator, in ourselves, which raises additional questions: *What stories do you tell the people in your life? How do you tell them? Why do you tell them when you tell them?* When we comprehend ourselves as both the protagonists of our own lives and the narrators of others' lives, we can grant ourselves new powers to tell different stories and also to live them.

SENSE AND SENSIBILITY

Every fine emotion produced in the reader has been,
and must have been, previously felt by the writer,
but in a far greater degree.

— ARNOLD BENNETT

AS YOU TELL YOUR STORY, focus on creating a rich sensory
and emotional experience, one that makes sense to readers so
they can more fully experience it. Do so because you'll never
abandon a draft that makes you feel, nor will your readers easily
set aside the book it may become.

From those principles conceived by fellow and past writers to serve readers — what we've previously called *craft* —
emerges a collective reverence for writing to the senses. Our
senses underpin the primal power of stories to make us feel.

More concretely, the senses act on both our bodies and our
imaginations, and they interact closely with our emotions. The
mere description of a eucalyptus leaf, for instance, can summon
up an otherwise remote aroma and texture, as well as memory-
borne sensations like nostalgia or exhilaration. Consider this
excerpt from Ian McEwan's novel *Saturday*:

There's a taste in the air, sweet and vaguely antiseptic, that reminds him of his teenage years in these streets and, of a general state of longing, a hunger for life to begin that from this distance seems like happiness.

And another from Junot Díaz's short story "Ysrael":

He'd punch me in the shoulder and walk on until what was left of him was the color of his shirt filling in the spaces between the leaves. Something inside of me would sag like a sail. I would yell his name and he'd hurry on, the ferns and branches and flower pods trembling in his wake.

As McEwan's and Diaz's words demonstrate, it's no accident that the word *sense* refers at once to clarity of understanding (as in something that "makes sense") and awareness of environment, whereas *sensibility* covers sensitivity to emotion and moral discernment. We need authors to pay attention to both sense and sensibility so we can at once lose and find ourselves as we read.

> We need authors to pay attention to both sense and sensibility so we can at once lose and find ourselves as we read.

When we understand its movements, a great story draws us into what novelist John Gardner describes as a "continuous narrative dream." An author's deft use of the senses — all eight of them, including kinesthetic (movement), vestibular (balance), and organic (such as hunger or thirst) — helps us vicariously experience strangers' love, grief, and pain to a degree that sometimes exceeds what we've felt in our own lives. Such stories also reveal to us depths we hadn't known we possessed — literature generally has a lighter touch than life, but stories and essays shape who we are in a similar way, by connecting us with events that alter our perspectives and make new reactions possible.

In order to stimulate your own and your readers' sensations and sensibilities, you need to raise the stakes on characters' desires and obstacles; root your narrative in a believable story world and setting; and apply judicious sensory detail to enliven and authenticate the geography that shapes destiny.

Just as great challenges in our own lives require a proportional commitment, we're more likely to devote ourselves to a character undertaking a grail quest than a stroll to the corner store. In the following excerpts, the authors deploy the senses, often subtly, to magnify reality and raise the stakes. In George Saunders's short story "Tenth of December," a young boy and an old man each risk death in an attempt to save each other: "The kid's pants were frozen solid. His boots were ice sculptures of boots." In his memoir *If I Die in a Combat Zone*, Tim O'Brien tells of how he can't bring himself to let down his community, so he goes to fight in Vietnam:

> By noon the next day our hands were in the air, even the tough guys. We recited the proper words, some of us loudly and daringly and others in bewilderment. It was a brightly lighted room, wood-paneled. A flag gave the place the right colors, there was some smoke in the air. We said the words, and we were soldiers.

In her travel memoir *Finding George Orwell in Burma*, the pseudonymous Emma Larkin draws on Orwell's facts and fictions to expose the horrors of life under the military junta without endangering the people who spoke with her:

He uncovered an old Penguin copy of *Animal Farm*. It had the familiar orange and white stripes on the cover, and yellowed pages that felt very slightly damp. He told me it was the first novel he had read in English. "It is a very brilliant book and it is a very Burmese book. Do you know why?" he asked, poking a finger enthusiastically in my general direction. "Because it is about pigs and dogs ruling the country!"

Ultimately, life-or-death stakes lay bare the underlying forces that drive characters, while use of the senses intensifies our involvement in the characters' lives.

As you draft, make sure that your characters' physical and emotional interactions with the places they inhabit shape your page-to-page plot. In many stories, the environment plays such a powerful role as to become a principal character in its own right, as in *The Perfect Storm*, *Breakfast at Tiffany's*, and *A Girl of the Limberlost*. Like water taking the shape of its container, stories both emerge from and adapt to their staging grounds, whether a Russian country estate (*The Cherry Orchard*), a Chicago public housing complex (*There Are No Children Here*), or a geisha district in Kyoto (*Memoirs of a Geisha*).

A realistic setting that we can see, smell, hear, touch, and even taste will also add greatly to the credibility of your story. Readers find Elizabeth George's British mystery novels so convincing that they're often surprised to discover that she's an American residing in Southern California. Writers living in the United Kingdom might find the research for a comparable series more convenient, but they must labor no less if they hope to make readers fully believe in the places they describe.

> A realistic setting that we can see, smell, hear, touch, and even taste will add greatly to the credibility of your story.

If it's a fictional place, it only needs to feel true, but if it's a real place, then it also needs to be accurate. A pioneer of African literature, Chinua Achebe rejected colonialist works that made readers feel by depicting his homeland in a false and negative, if vivid, light. "It began to dawn on me that although fiction was undoubtedly fictitious it could also be true or false, not with the truth or falsehood of a news item but as to its disinterestedness, its intention, its integrity," he wrote. When you work with feelings, you also need to exercise good sense. As Pablo Picasso observed, "Art is a lie that helps us to see the truth." When we write fiction, we're permitted to sacrifice lesser truths in order to create moving and thought-provoking illusions, but we should do so with the aim of revealing greater truths.

As you draft, you're striving to bring illusions to the page, but these same illusions can help you create if you're prepared to exercise your imagination in a new way. A strong sense of place, for instance, might enable you to compensate for the tyranny of the unknown that reigns over all those yet-to-be-written pages. In the television series *Battlestar Galactica*, the alien Cylons possess such powers of projection that they can perceive themselves in a forest or on a beach when they're actually walking the bland corridors of their base ship.

Each day you draft, you confront the void of the blank page, yet you have the same power to imagine that void giving way to the world of your story, whether you're witness to a group of uniformed officers approaching you across the interlocking decks and corridors of a light-speed vessel or a Jesus lizard in flight from a predator, making a mad dash across the surface of an Amazon river. Let images subsume the white space onto which you type, and spill out across your desk, onto your floor. Take it further and step directly into the world you're creating. Open yourself to the full sensory experience of events making their way onto your pages. And feel your way onward.

BEGIN WITH WHAT YOU KNOW

Don't just write what you know;
write what you don't know
then learn about it.

— ELIZABETH ENGSTROM

ALL PROJECTS REQUIRE some form of research, whether that means sifting through a library's archives or just the archives of your own mind. Research best serves drafting, however, when you begin with what you already know, interrupting your writing only to seek out what you *need* when you need it.

Here we reinterpret the truism "Write what you know" as a check against fact-finding run amok. The great explorer Ulysses, when he speaks to us through Alfred, Lord Tennyson's poem, captures something of the yearning that every writer feels to step away from the dream just as the time comes to draft: "Yet all experience is an arch wherethro' / Gleams that untravell'd world." Stopper your ears to this siren song and stay on course.

In the Draft stage, we urge you to limit any research you do as much as possible so as to devote the bulk of your energies to telling your story. You can always insert brackets as placeholders for details yet to come. That's not to say you can't gather useful information during this stage. Just make sure that any necessary research takes place in parallel to — and not in place of — drafting, and that it derives focus from the story you've defined. This principle holds true whether you're writing a biography, a fantasy novel, or anything in between, though the amount and kind of research needed will differ.

> **Make sure that any necessary research takes place in parallel to drafting, and that it derives focus from the story you've defined.**

When Geraldine Brooks, for instance, began research on her novel *Caleb's Crossing*, she'd already defined crucial points of the story she wanted to tell — that of Harvard's first Native American graduate in 1665. She also knew that she'd have to compensate for written history's neglect:

> I talked with tribal members, read translations of early documents in the Wopanaak language, then delved into the archives of Harvard and the Massachusetts Bay Colony....I read the correspondence between colonial leaders and benefactors in England who donated funds for the education and conversion to Christianity of Indians in the 17th century.

Already an experienced novelist and a journalist before that, Brooks carried out the broad-based investigation necessary to bring Caleb's world to life, but she never stopped looking for resources that would point her more directly toward story: "Throughout the research, my dream was that this big stack of documents or a journal written by Caleb would emerge." It never did.

The heart of her fictional work, however, sprang from what

she could and did know, thanks to Caleb's only surviving arti-
fact: in a letter written in Latin by the unlikely young scholar
and addressed to his English Christian patrons, he touched on
the myth of Orpheus, who'd made a crossing between worlds
that he compared with his own.

As Brooks's work on *Caleb's Crossing* demonstrates, historical novels require the author to determine how research can best
support drafting and how atmospheric detail can enrich story.
In contrast, the novelist immersed in the emotional essence of
a contemporary work of fiction, anchored only in her imagination, may need to employ an alternate stratagem in order to
continue moving forward. In *The Secret Miracle: The Novelist's Handbook*, Curtis Sittenfeld relates an "excellent piece of
advice" she took from fellow novelist Mona Simpson:

> I'm paraphrasing, but she basically said you should
> write up to the point when you know exactly what infor-
> mation you need.... So you write a scene, and you have
> two characters having an argument about ice hockey,
> but you know nothing about ice hockey. You put X's
> or TK's or other placeholders in for their dialogue, but
> you write the rest of the scene. Then you go and find
> someone who does know something about ice hockey
> and ask them what your characters should be saying.

The technique that Sittenfeld describes will help you put
your story first, letting the cascading train of research bring up
the rear, because the facts must serve the story, even if they do
so differently in fiction and nonfiction. The placeholders that
Sittenfeld employs also serve another purpose: they remind us

that we're not expected to know everything in the Draft stage and that we are prepared, all the same, to begin with what we know.

When you do find time to venture beyond your desk, actually talking with people can provide an infusion of energy that you'll take back to your draft. When conducting interviews, you'll find another fluid starting point in the principle around which this chapter revolves. Most people are inherently anxious and insecure as to their own expertise and ability to communicate it. You can reassure them by beginning with what they know.

Research that seeks out story, along with facts, is all the more likely to find it.

You might open the conversation with the easy questions: Where did you grow up? What's the first thing you do each morning? With whom do you enjoy collaborating? These questions and others like them will also offer your subject opportunities to tell stories, and most of us love to tell stories, especially to an appreciative audience. From this limited example comes a more generally applicable truth: research that seeks out story, along with facts, is all the more likely to find it.

As previously stated, some genres do require more advance research than others. We're not recommending that you plunge into your biography or historical novel about, say, Harriet Tubman, with only basic knowledge of her life. We're urging you to trust in and to follow the thread of your own interest — to begin with what you know about the subject, what originally arrested your attention, so that you can make a coherent journey from there into the unknown. You're a pearl diver who seeks to unearth that singular treasure and then return with it as quickly as possible.

If you go about it the right way, your research can support

and not disrupt your drafting efforts. And the more you recognize the constraints that shape your story, the more targeted your research must become. As you review relevant books or documents, some questions will help you make the most of that work while remaining focused on your own:

❖ What parts of this work bring you closest to its central meaning?

❖ What other contribution does the remainder of the text make?

❖ What sources did the author of this book or document draw on for his research? Might any of these sources (e.g., maps or court records) benefit your work?

❖ What literary techniques has the author employed to enliven factual information or to navigate gaps in the historical record? How might you do the same?

You'll recognize your line of inquiry as effective when it pulls you deeper into your story and not away from it.

"Which way is deeper?" you might well ask. Another good question — one that only you can answer with regard to your particular project. We've already pointed the way in general, whereas now you'll make it out more precisely: head as directly as possible toward your story's central meaning as defined during the Dream stage.

It's a feeling and an instinct that you can augment by observing yourself and by synthesizing your past experiences through reflection; you may find it useful to turn back to notes, journal entries, or dialogues with yourself that you wrote down while defining your story. We also encourage you to consult with fellow writers, either in conversation or by reading in-depth interviews with them. Consider the acknowledgments in related books, which may point to the kind of research authors did, and at what point, when working on a comparable project.

Bear in mind: others' experience can inform your writing practice, but it shouldn't supersede what works for you. Keep dreaming in dialogue so as to track the development of your own process and to draw clear connections between your research and your story. And above all, keep on drafting.

In deciding to begin with what you know, you surrender fully to that magical transition between sitting down with no idea what you're going to write and, perhaps moments later, putting words on the page. First you don't know, and then you do, and — yes, you can finally grasp it on looking back — you always know more than you think you do.

SIERRA: HOW TO LISTEN

Good listeners are not only popular everywhere,
but after a while they learn something.

— WILSON MIZNER

I REMEMBER THE FIRST TIME I recognized the role that silence
plays in conversation. I needed both hands to type up my interviews for the *Stanford Daily*, and I recall the awkwardness of the
corded phone, tucked between my left ear and shoulder. "Uh-
huh," I said, my fast-moving fingers trailing the faster-moving
words of the varsity sailing coach. I'd been assigned the obituary
of a young alumnus, a skier who'd died in an avalanche. When
the coach stopped speaking, I had to focus on taking down what
he'd just said and couldn't immediately ask another question.
Into the unintended silence came the story that I needed, something we should remember about Jeremy David McIntyre:

> In the final race of our qualifying for nationals, a high-
> pressure event...we got into a protest...over one of
> the rules on the water, meaning that somebody gets dis-
> qualified. The other guy [in the protest] is one of his
> best friends from Longhorn [Texas]. I've never seen a

guy cry over winning a protest, but he won it, and he
got to go to nationals, and his friend didn't.

If I'd immediately asked another question, the coach might
have been too busy answering it to recall this story. Like most
people, he seemed to find in silence the impetus to speak, and,
after a pause, he resumed talking and the anecdote I'd been seeking emerged. We all do what we can to fill silence,
and often it means abruptly finding the words
to continue when, only a heartbeat before,
we believed there were none. I realized
then that as a journalist, I could make
use of others' discomfort with silence to
prevail on them to speak. I felt comfortable doing so because, most of the time, the
people I interview share my objective: to tell
a true and meaningful story.

> **We all do
> what we can to fill
> silence, and often it means
> abruptly finding the words
> to continue when, only a
> heartbeat before, we
> believed there
> were none.**

I haven't feared silence since I became acquainted with its
sublime power when I acted in school plays. No matter the play,
I learned, great drama invariably accompanies that brief hush
in the break between house lights going down and stage lights
coming up and that moment just before the audience begins to
applaud.

During each performance, when the actors fell silent, even
if only for a beat, we could feel the presence of the spectators as
intensely as if they stood directly behind us, gently breathing
upon the backs of our necks. When we spoke, they listened, and
we spoke because they listened. When we paused, they waited,
and we felt the tension of their anticipation as though it were a
golden thread leading us forward.

As a journalist and teacher, I feel a similar connection to

the people with whom I work, and I put that connection first. When interviewing, I generate specific questions in the moment and rely on a recorder for face-to-face meetings because I want to be able to make eye contact with my subjects as often as feels natural. In the classroom, I try to find a balance between treating students as a group and attending to them as individuals. In each case, I take part in a strange kind of conversation, strange because it's a conversation in which I speak as little as possible — though not necessarily as little as I'd prefer.

At my best, I resemble a giant ear, alert and skeptical, yet nonjudgmental because I'm taking the opportunity to consider the world from the speaker's perspective. When I say anything, I ask all sorts of questions, especially the silly ones, because they sometimes elicit serious answers, and those answers tell me what to ask next.

Sometimes I say nothing and just listen, because silence can be the most effective question. It's what we all hear when we're alone, and it's when our dreams and fears emerge from the shadows and whisper to us. We resist silence, but we're also drawn to it, as the peaceful, closed-lipped smile of the Buddha attests. We seek to fill the silence with words and stories, but silence also takes up residence in those stories — in moments of revelation and in blank space and punctuation markers that form the equivalent of musical rests. Silence gives stories meaning that words alone cannot.

When we sit down with the blank page, we let the initial silence form a simple question: *What am I going to write now?*

Now I see that these overlapping, interlocking experiences lie at the heart of the writer's work, especially the Draft stage. When we sit down with the blank page, we willingly submit to the vast space within and without, and we let the initial silence form a simple question: *What am I going to write now?* Writing — like teaching, reporting, performing, and so many other disciplines — requires us to listen. We're listening to our own voices. We're listening to the voices of others. We're listening to the world around us. When I think of myself as listening while I write, I bring a sense of patience to my own work that makes progress in stages possible.

When I wrote my first book, *Creative Lives*, profiling Lebanese artists, I became aware of myself as listening differently at different points in my own process. During thirty-one interviews, I paid careful attention to what each person said, without thinking about what I would write; if I'd already known what I intended to write, then there'd have been little point to an interview. With each question, I felt as though I were laying down a stepping-stone, oriented by the speaker's answer to the preceding question. When I sat down to take notes from the recorded conversation, I listened for what interested me, confident that it would also interest my future readers. When I drafted, I listened for what mattered most, selecting some event or idea that might plunge the reader directly into the center of each subject's life. And when I developed and refined, I listened to my readers, both real and imaginary, guessing at the questions they might ask and endeavoring to answer them in the text.

And now, a few years later, I listen to what I remember: Filmmaker Joana Hadjithomas said she encouraged her students to pay attention to what they admired, that admiration is important. Composer Guy Manoukian told me that a melody had to "bug him" before he'd consent to work with it. Architect Nabil Gholam said that at some point, he decided to "worry again about that white sheet" of paper and all the possibilities he might be missing. Composer Khaled Mouzanar told me that he discovered he could compose because he kept failing to imitate others' melodies. And sculptor Anachar Basbous said that every one of his pieces harmonized the original inspiration with the creative freedom he permitted himself during each day of the work.

I keep listening to these and other voices from the past and present because the stories don't change, but I do. I listen, knowing that others' experience will give me some idea of my own, if only because, in everything we do, we're all listening to one another.

HOW TO READ WRITING BOOKS

Everything that needs to be said
has already been said.
But since no one was listening,
everything must be said again.

— ANDRÉ GIDE

ONCE YOU FINISH THIS CHAPTER, or stage, put this book down, and don't take it up again until you've first taken some time to draft — or, if you're not currently working on a project, to write in search of one. Even just fifteen minutes. Then come on back. Why? Because something amazing happens when you move back and forth between reading and actually applying what you've learned to your own work. And that's what it's all about, right? Reading while writing; reading in order to write more, better, truer.

At this stage in particular, we know you'll be tempted to set aside drafting for so-called educational reading. It's a habit we all form in our school days: study now, achieve later. When we bring this old routine to our current writing, it can become a crutch because it means we stop producing pages. We often tell ourselves we just need a little guidance when actually we want something else: permission to write at all, authority to write well, and inspiration to begin doing so right now.

It's writing now, however, more than reading, that's needed to prove to you that lasting permission, authority, and inspiration can come only from the practice itself. Your practice. When you read while writing and invite the two to interact with each other, you're refusing to settle for a mere feeling of inspiration or the suggestion that words of wisdom will inevitably prove valuable, and to you in particular. Far better to go with experiment-tested reality.

Lasting permission, authority, and inspiration can come only from the practice itself.

But what does it mean for your reading and writing to "interact with each other"? It's a concrete practice in itself. As you read this or any writing guidebook, underline those sentences that speak to you — whereas in school you may have underlined only to identify the author's most salient points in order to fulfill an assignment. Fill up the margins with notes. Or dedicate a separate notebook to the task so as to more directly engage with the wider body of knowledge on writing and story craft that each guide approaches from a different angle. Note down your first impressions of new ways of thinking or techniques; comment on comparable or contrasting ideas in other books; and flag those passages that contain an approach you want to try out in your own work as soon as possible. Then go and try them out.

A technique that doesn't work for you today may turn out to be immensely useful two years down the line. All the more reason for you to think of yourself as accumulating a personal library that tracks with and reflects your own creative development. Maybe one day, you'll organize your writing books autobiographically just as Rob Gordon memorably did with his records in Nick Hornby's novel *High Fidelity*. As Gordon put it (in the film version):

> I can tell you how I got from *Deep Purple* to *Howlin' Wolf* in just twenty-five moves and if I want to find the song "Landslide" by Fleetwood Mac, I have to remember that I bought it for someone in the fall of 1983 pile but didn't give it to them for personal reasons.

In your own library, you'll find the ghosts of your past selves, a group you'll want to consult whenever you write memoir or personal history. You'll also preserve a record of your own evolution through time. This library will come to include books from many genres, especially those genres in which you write. In fact, *every* book is a writing book to the extent that the author has made choices that may inform yours. Just don't forget that any published text reveals only the author's final layer of decisions and not all the wayward impulses that likely preceded it and that define the Draft stage. You can still learn by evaluating the effectiveness of what each author settled upon.

Every book is a writing book to the extent that the author has made choices that may inform yours.

The more you analyze others' work while drafting your own, the more you'll become aware of the author as a kind of spectral presence. You can turn even long-dead writers into bona fide mentors by rereading their work in tandem with their biography or, at minimum, their Wikipedia page.

Though works of literature can become timeless as far as readers are concerned, each of these works first emerged from a particular person at a particular moment in time — a useful reminder to the practicing writer, who herself lives at a particular moment in time. A biography not only situates an author in history but may include excerpts of his early drafts; correspondence in which the author confided his own doubts and struggles; and commentaries about what he read and how it influenced his own writing.

Both Stephen King and the young-adult author Avi have suggested that aspiring writers should make it a point to read so-called bad books along with good ones. At the least, as King says, you'll put down the book thinking, "I can do better than this. Hell, I *am* doing better than this!" You'll also find it easier to recognize not only what does work but also what doesn't work — so you can avoid or excise it later.

Do you feel indignant because a character acted irrationally or the plot took an unjustifiable turn? Feelings like these will force you out of the text and into the realization that the author could have made a different choice, something you may not appreciate while fully absorbed in a well-crafted work.

It's easier to analyze stories on rereading them, or films when you see them a second time, but remember that it takes effort to keep your head when the whole purpose of story is for you to lose it. With your pen in hand and your project firmly in mind, imagine that you might pull the next incarnation of your story right through the text in front of you, as though it were a magician's rabbit emerging from a silken top hat, its nose wiggling, its velvet body throbbing with life.

WRITING AS A SOLITARY ACT

Writers must be alone, uninterrupted,
and slightly savage if they are to
sustain and complete an undertaking.

— JESSAMYN WEST

YOU MAY NEVER FEEL more alone than when you draft. When your manuscript is more idea than reality, you have little choice but to put your dreams on a subsistence diet of will and hope. In the depths of this aloneness lies the risk of loneliness but also the potential for solitude, a small kind of salvation.

Some of us, like the thesaurus, treat *solitude* and *loneliness* as synonyms: editor Malcolm Campbell, for instance, described "acceptance of solitude" as the "writer's first duty," and Pablo Picasso dubbed solitude the "price the artist pays" for "time to see, to think, to learn, to practice, and to express." Solitude can seem a duty or a price. But, with just a little ingenuity, it can become an opportunity.

When novelist and playwright Honoré de Balzac occupied an austere, unheated garret, he inscribed on one wall the words "Rosewood paneling"; on another, "Gobelin tapestry with Venetian mirror"; and directly over the empty fireplace, he wrote, "Painting by Raphael." With a simple yet sweeping change in perspective, he at once made light of and triumphed over his poverty. At the least, as he demonstrated, solitude boasts superior furnishing to loneliness.

More generally, consider two people who go without food for several days: one states contentedly that he's "fasting," and the other reports miserably that he's "starving." Fasting is voluntary; starvation is not. Even as circumstances differ, the point remains the same: *loneliness* heralds an involuntary feeling of isolation, while *solitude* signifies a voluntary state of pleasure in one's own company. When lonely, we suffer, seemingly intent on plumbing the depths of our own deprivation; when solitary, we can savor an intensity that grounds us within ourselves so that we may eventually find self-transcendence.

> *Solitude* signifies a voluntary state of pleasure in one's own company.

Poet Carl Sandburg saw clearly: "Without great solitude no serious work is possible." Inventor Nikola Tesla, likewise, once stated that the mind is "sharper and keener in seclusion." As these two don't quite make clear, however, solitude is a practice, not a prescription. We need to learn *how* to inhabit this seclusion by choosing aloneness when we could have chosen otherwise, then seeing what we can make of it and watching ourselves do so.

Modern living creates another layer of difficulty, but if the need to create is great enough, even the busiest schedules accommodate. While still a practicing attorney with a punishing schedule, novelist David Baldacci managed to write after his wife went to sleep. Jean M. Auel, in contrast, had to contend with working full-time and attending graduate school at night, not to mention all that raising five children entailed, when she drafted the first book in a bestselling series, *The Clan of the Cave Bear*. To Baldacci and Auel, any possibility of uninterrupted aloneness probably started to look a lot like solitude.

As you make solitude part of your life, you'll come to appreciate it as a sanctuary within your own mind, an intangible space that nonetheless has tangible effects. In an address to the plebe class at West Point, author and essayist William Deresiewicz described how solitude makes it possible for those who possess it to clearly hear their own voices amid "the stream of other people's thoughts." He defines solitude in terms of "introspection," "the concentration of focused work," "sustained reading" — and, most counterintuitively, "the deep friendship of intimate conversation." Even as we write alone, this last meaning holds particular relevance for us because we never truly write alone.

> You'll come to appreciate solitude as a sanctuary within your own mind, an intangible space that nonetheless has tangible effects.

In solitude, writers, thinkers, and artists tap into a limitless world of imagination; we commune with fellow creators, past and present, what author and traveler Paul Watkins has called the "fellowship of ghosts"; and we sense those who may one day encounter our stories and be transported by them as we have been moved by the work of others.

Through the voices of our characters, which grow more and more coherent as we draft, we discover new dimensions in our own voice. Further afield, in our awareness of a shared labor, we find a buoy: at any given moment, all over the world, countless other writers are also drafting, as well as dreaming, developing, and refining — each one of us laboring in solitude together.

At last we know for sure: true solitude is no sacrifice. It's the community of one that enables us to create in the first place.

DAN: THE WILL TO WRITE

The art of writing is the art of applying
the seat of the pants to the seat of the chair.

— MARY HEATON VORSE

THIRTY YEARS AGO, after writing two mediocre drafts of a book, I began to despair that I might ever compose anything of value. I sank into the doldrums, a sailing ship on a windless sea. I tried to convince myself that there was nothing wrong with not writing. As Julian Barnes observed, "It is easy not to be a writer. Most people are not writers, and very little harm comes to them because of it." Charles Grodin's advice to aspiring actors also spoke to me: "If you can do anything else, then go do it. If you can't, then you might make it."

I certainly tried to do other things. I put in hours at a nine-to-five administrative job, then went home to my family. In my spare time, I went for walks or to the movies. In short, I busied myself with the rest of life.

But I couldn't *not* write, at least not for very long. In retrospect, I can relate to what choreographer George Balanchine once said: "I don't look for people who want to dance; I look for people who need to dance." That same need or passion that drove Balanchine's dancers moved me to return to the keyboard and to face the fact that it might never get any easier. My years in gymnastics had taught me that a wish or need to write would not by itself propel me into the work any more than a desire to get into better shape automatically translates into a regular workout routine.

Every time I sat down to write, I had to set my will against doubt and inertia. But then again, so did John Steinbeck, who wrote, "When I face the desolate impossibility of writing five hundred pages, a sick sense of failure falls onto me, and I know I can never do it. Then gradually, I write one page, then another. One day's work is all I can permit myself to contemplate."

At this point, I decided, for the first time, to develop a regular writing routine. I sat down at the same time each day. As much as I might have welcomed a call from a friend, I turned off the phone because even a brief distraction could wreck any momentum I'd generated. During a daily thirty-minute warm-up period, I made my way into writing time, which had to remain sacred, just like my former training sessions in the gymnasium. I needed to become my own protagonist, slaying dragons on the way to my goals.

Fixing on a clear, achievable goal during each session has anchored my will to write.

I returned to drafting. Initially, I aimed to write for a specific number of hours each day, but then I set my sights on a certain number of words. The first goal ultimately helped me develop the stamina that I needed to accomplish the second. When all else fails, I remind myself that I only have to write one word, one sentence, and one page at a time. Whatever my evolving method, fixing on a clear, achievable goal during each session has anchored my will to write.

Seneca once said, "The Fates lead those who will. Those

who won't, they drag." Some days, inspiration takes hold as soon as I set out. Other days, I have to drag myself through the entire session. Satirist Peter De Vries quipped, "I only write when I'm inspired — and I see to it that I'm inspired at nine o'clock every morning." Jack London put it even more emphatically: "Don't loaf and invite inspiration. Light after it with a club."

I've since written sixteen published books. I keep on writing because I've learned to distinguish between two fundamental approaches to achieving my goals:

I can strive to create empowering beliefs, work on my self-esteem, and practice positive self-talk to focus my mind and affirm my power to visualize desired outcomes so as to acquire the confidence to generate the courage to find the determination to make the commitment to feel sufficiently motivated to get down to work.

Or I can just do it.

I chose the second road. I choose it every day, and that has made all the difference.

PERMIT YOURSELF
TO WRITE BADLY

One day, when I was agonizing over
how utterly bad my writing felt, I realized:
That's actually not my problem.
I never promised the universe that I would write brilliantly;
I only promised the universe that I would write.
So I put my head down and sweated through it,
as per my vows.

— ELIZABETH GILBERT

WHAT WE CALL WRITER'S BLOCK usually stems from a lack of perspective about the nature of the drafting process. No matter how many paroxysms of doubt or crises of confidence we endure, they're rarely sufficient in themselves to physically stop us from putting words on the page. Let's admit it together: in moments of literary paralysis, nothing blocks us except ourselves. Nobody forces us away from our keyboards and out of our chairs. No poltergeist wrestles the pen from our hands. We choose to stop writing, or not to begin, because we don't believe our words are good enough, which must mean we're not good enough. And never will be good enough. Ever. *How dare you write another sentence*, an inner voice intones, *knowing it will only manifest itself as more damning evidence of your mediocrity?*

Alas, in such cases, your writing has become Important, even if only the pages in front of you. Everything else you've written has faded into the background like unobtrusive wallpaper. The middling text you're generating at that moment — and it's never just bad, it's *terrible, the worst writing in the world!* — has become exhibit A, both murder weapon and suicide note. Your inner prosecutor is happy to play along: *That's shit. Do you hear me? Pure shit. No, not Hemingway's "The first draft of anything is shit"* — *actual* shit.

Believing ourselves blocked, we become imaginary invalids, so we need an imaginary antidote. Fortunately, there's one at hand: we must grant ourselves permission to write badly. Why? Because we're *supposed* to write badly in the Draft stage. That's right. It's our duty.

The first draft requires a show of sinew, not nuance. We write badly because we need our early drafts to show us, in broad strokes, what we're actually supposed to be writing about. We write badly because we need to focus our energy on the larger story and structure, and can't possibly attend to all the elements that make up a developed or refined work. We write badly because, even if we revise as we draft — and, mea culpa, many of us do — either we can't revise with a complete manuscript in mind or we're too close to that manuscript to have sufficient perspective. We write badly at first because our early drafts should look bad in retrospect and because they force us to earn the experience and pay the dues that make progress possible. It's a shame, but reaching a higher point always means

> We're *supposed* to write badly in the Draft stage. That's right. It's our duty.

that we had to inhabit a lower one at some earlier time. In the end, we also have to be able to acknowledge that something we create might be bad — without it meaning that *everything* we create will be bad.

So when you draft, depress your expectations, not yourself. You'll draft and then you'll develop. With each rewrite, you can permit your standards to climb that much more, until it's time to refine and you can unleash your inner perfectionist. That's not to say that every draft (or every book) will be better than the last — you can make progress more likely but not inevitable. Regardless, drafting means recognizing that even something bad holds value for you, all the more so if it means you'll keep on writing, even if only because you know you'll eventually circle back and make it better.

There may be no better time to commit to writing than when it's going badly. As any experienced author will tell you, we prove ourselves in times of crisis not by writing well but by writing onward. "A bad day," Sylvia Plath wrote in one journal entry. "A bad time. State of mind most important for work. A blithe, itchy eager state where the poem itself, the story itself is supreme."

> **We prove ourselves in times of crisis not by writing well but by writing onward.**

At one point in her career, Madeleine L'Engle probably wouldn't have agreed. She'd published two books, but it had been years since she'd received anything but rejections from publishers. So, on her fortieth birthday, she decided to quit, shrouded her typewriter, and paced, weeping:

I stopped in my tracks because my subconscious mind was blip, blip, blip, blipping up to my conscious mind the plot of a novel on failure. So I uncovered the typewriter. That night I wrote in my journal "I have to write. That's the gift I've been given. And even if I am never, ever published again it is still what I have to do."…

I'm glad that I made that decision about myself as a writer in the moment of utter darkness [because it's] easy to say you're a writer when your books are being published and making money, but I wasn't being published, and I wasn't making any money. So it was a very real decision. And it is a decision we all have to make.

Four years later, and after a lot more rejection, L'Engle published *A Wrinkle in Time*. "It was a dark and stormy night," the story begins. Indeed, sometimes it is. But even when rejected, dejected, and feeling blocked, we can choose to go on. Make it a mantra: *Get it done first — get it right later.* Turn your back on your inner prosecutor and declare each effort *good enough for now*. The defense rests.

FIRST DRAFT, FIRST LAYER

We do not grow absolutely, or chronologically.
We are made up of layers, cells, constellations.

— ANAÏS NIN

IF WE WERE THERE TO WITNESS the precise moment when you finished telling your story on paper, we'd clap you on the back — and then we'd tell you that you're finally ready to begin. We'd tell you (and, in fact, we are telling you) that the real work of the writer lies not in completing one draft but in making significant jumps from one draft to the next, what we call development.

Before you can move forward to the Develop stage, however, you need to understand just why you'll be able to pull forth a stronger draft from the body of your first draft, not to mention each subsequent draft — because every creative work comes together in layers, even all those classics you read in school. Especially those classics.

At this point, it's easier to recognize that the five stages are not strictly linear; they're also cyclical. In Draft, you've made an initial attempt to tell your story. Before that, you dreamed up, expanded, and elaborated on the sticky idea that gave rise to it, returning to that idea and reworking it as you defined your story. At the next stage, in the next chapter, you'll go over the same body of text again and again; only it won't remain the same because you'll *develop* it.

At this point, you need to reconceive your earliest draft as forming the first material layer of your story. That layer will dissolve into each additional layer, itself a reflection of another round of major craft decisions. Readers of any published work will only perceive the contribution made by the last layer of the author's decisions, but authors will recall the labyrinth now concealed within that work, the passages that led nowhere, the paths not taken. In an interview with Terri Gross, the actor and author Ethan Hawke made a pertinent comment when he discussed the years of conversation between collaborators that went into drafting the film *Before Midnight*, the third in a series: "The fun of these movies is they get to gestate over nine years. I mean, we get to have really in-depth ideas that we can throw away, but they're not gone, they became a coat of paint."

Reconceive your earliest draft as forming the first material layer of your story.

It's easier to grasp the mechanics of drafting in layers on looking back — and on looking again — so let's approach this topic from another angle: Imagine you've already produced a short written work from several drafts, each of which incorporated substantial changes. Can you see those drafts stacked in front of you, ordered from first to last? Flip through them, watching as changes to the text flash by: sentences falling away or materializing; paragraphs taking on new expression and order; ideas appearing from nothing and gradually emerging from obscurity into clarity.

But what makes such alterations to the text productive? They need to carry out larger decisions that support the story's over-arching elements: structure, plot, character, story world, setting, and theme. Why invest energy in crafting elegant sentences when you may cut the paragraphs, or even the whole chapter, in which they're embedded because they don't serve your story? It's most important in Draft and Develop that your sentences convey essential ideas; they don't yet need to do so perfectly.

For that reason, don't let the details distract you. Stay loyal to and focused on the story you haven't yet fully incarnated — the story that has already guided the choices you've made on the page and that will continue to guide your progress. At its most specific, preparing for development requires you to assess whether your draft has deviated from the story you set out to tell and whether drafting has exposed flaws in that original idea. In order to review your draft with this second sight, you'll probably need to physically step away from your desk for a period of time — as long as it takes you to ensure that you'll be reading afresh rather than remembering your manuscript when you return to it.

If you're on deadline or just feel compelled to push on without a major respite, there are other ways to cultivate distance from the work. One of the easiest and most accessible: Read your work aloud, either to yourself or to someone else. Read it as though you were performing it — and observe the gap that opens when you become actor more than author. Some large department stores offer coffee beans in their fragrance sections because the smell of the beans clears the palate and enables focus on one perfume at a time. As you get to know your way of working, why not look for your own coffee

> **Read your work aloud and observe the gap that opens when you become actor more than author.**

beans? What activity or experience might enable you to spend the minimum amount of time away from a work while still recalibrating your perspective to a sufficient degree?

You may determine that a long walk, a few games of solitaire, an hour or two spent playing a musical instrument or cleaning, or getting a good night's sleep will recalibrate your perspective to a meaningful degree. You can also take a more methodical approach, rereading earlier notes or dialogues to assess whether what you've drafted fulfills the aims you've laid out for it or whether these aims have changed.

At this point, the comments of a fellow writer or astute reader can also generate a shift in perspective. Any confusion your early readers express will expose the gap between your own experience of the story as drafted and the reader's ability to engage with it. When you think of yourself as drafting in layers, you recognize that an early reader's confusion can reorient you and point toward a specific direction in which to revise.

When you work on a manuscript over months or years, in service to a sticky idea that has remained meaningful, something marvelous happens. Through the writing, you discover what continues to matter to you, no matter the passing of time. You tap into a deeper, more resilient layer within yourself, the bedrock below the flowing river. When you complete your first draft, you reach a turning point and a moment of self-recognition that are worth savoring, even after you've begun to develop. You understand the value of both looking again — at your work, at yourself — and of that first long look, that earliest layer. You know that the second look won't make the first any less true in its own time, just as your older self will never make your younger self any less real.

A trip becomes a journey
after you have lost your luggage.

— ANONYMOUS

INTRODUCTION

THE DEVELOP STAGE, more than any other, enables you to make significant creative leaps and earn valuable experience as you restructure and rewrite your manuscript so that it better embodies your story. We call development the *missing link* because many of us otherwise move directly from drafting to refining and wonder why we haven't made much progress.

You'll never again mistake lack of experience with lack of potential once you understand how sweat trumps talent and identify your Master Metaphor, which brings new confidence in your own abilities and prospects. We'll tell you how our Master Metaphors have developed.

You'll learn practical methods that support this stage's objective: follow the golden thread that defines the essential trajectory of your story. We show you how to gain distance from your words on the page while maintaining allegiance to your story, and how to connect voice and character in a way that enables you to strengthen both. Feedback becomes a spur to momentum and progress when you formulate and answer specific questions. In coming to grips with this most intensive stage, you'll find inspiration when — glimpsed anew through the lens of your story — the world becomes your teacher.

THE MISSING LINK

Works of art are always the result
of one's having been in danger,
of having gone through an experience
all the way to the end,
where no one can go any further.

— RAINER MARIA RILKE

EARLY IN *Drawing on the Right Side of the Brain*, art teacher and author Betty Edwards asks her readers to copy a van Gogh sketch printed upside down, further instructing them not to turn it right side up until they've finished. If you do this exercise and take proper care, your drawing will achieve a striking resemblance to van Gogh's. On taking a second look, however, you'll have little choice but to conclude that what separates the masters from you cannot be manual skill but is instead a way of seeing and sensing manifold possibilities where others perceive few or none.

In fact, every time you ask another person to take a "second look" at something, you acknowledge that, at times, all of us can look again and see the same thing in a new way, understand it differently. If you want to tell great stories, you need to learn how to apply this everyday skill to your work, to rewrite or revise — from the Latin *revisere*, "to look at again." But don't take our word for it; just ask John Irving, who said, "More than half, maybe as much as two-thirds of my life as a writer is rewriting." Or E. B. White: "I rewrite a good deal to make it clear." Or Elmore Leonard: "If it sounds like writing, I rewrite it." Or Vladimir Nabokov: "I have rewritten often several times, every word I have ever published." Or Supreme Court justice Louis Brandeis, who ruled, in a manner of speaking, "There is no great writing, only great rewriting." Or Ernest Hemingway, who rewrote the ending to *A Farewell to Arms* no fewer than forty-seven times before he felt satisfied — or just gave up.

The words *revise* and *rewrite*, however, indicate a need for change without specifying what change exactly. "Something… different, please!" they seem to say.

"But what?" you may ask. "Is there a script for this kind of thing?"

Yes and no — fittingly, what script we can consult comes to us from the world of film. Experienced writers know to differentiate between a developmental edit and a copyedit (and we'll get to that in a later chapter), but only screenwriters routinely talk about *developing* their own work. When they do, they formally acknowledge one important gap confronting all writers, a profound distance between the words on the page and the underlying (or overarching) story. Screenwriters can recognize this gap more easily because they write for production and not for readers. More a blueprint than a text, the screenplay serves as an intermediary between the dream and the film, which itself must go through the equivalent of dreaming and drafting (read: scouting and shooting), as well as development and refinement.

Storytellers, novelists, and expository writers need to realize that this gap also applies to their work: early drafts of an essay or a novel in progress point toward a concluding text, but they don't yet fully incarnate it. That's where development comes in — it's the missing link between vision and manifestation, between drafting and refinement, and, as we explored in the last chapter, between successive drafts or layers.

That's where development comes in — it's the missing link between vision and manifestation.

Jennifer Egan's experience with her first novel perfectly illustrates the gap between the words on the page and the story they may or may not convey, as well as the demands that gap can place on a writer. Years before she won the Pulitzer Prize, Egan told the website Opening Lines, she drafted a novel that "everyone hated" — but the original sticky idea would hold her allegiance. On picking up her manuscript again after a few years, she had a revelation:

> I'd so utterly missed the mark, that in a way I felt like I hadn't really touched the idea that I had wanted to deal with. It felt like I had just kind of aimed in the wrong direction and the target was still there and that made me want to give it another try. So I essentially threw [the original manuscript] out. I can't really say I rewrote it, because I didn't save a single word, but there were certain basic impulses and plot moves that really fueled the next attempt, and they were the same as the first in some ways. And that is what ultimately became the first novel that I published, *The Invisible Circus*.

Egan had to be able to see that revising her manuscript meant not just rewriting it but reinventing it. Terms like *revise* and *rewrite*, as Egan's experience show, can direct the writer's attention only to what's already been written — as though the initial mass of words amounts to a mess of puzzle pieces that simply need rearranging. Development, in contrast, allows for the possibility that a draft may actually need to expand, grow, and evolve.

Experienced professionals know that it's neither sufficient nor particularly productive, at this stage, to eliminate a dangling participle here, or correct a spelling error there, or quibble with oneself over synonyms. Before you move forward to the Refine stage, you may need to do any or all of the following: replace weaker ideas with stronger ones; restructure your work altogether, shifting paragraphs or entire sections for greater logic and effect; incorporate flashbacks or combine characters to streamline plot; and resolve inconsistencies that threaten the coherence of your narrative.

When it comes to your story, as well as yourself, not all growth need be visible. Developing a draft means making it deeper and richer without necessarily making it longer. When Ernest Hemingway developed, he pruned to make his text more concise and the stories that emerged from them more suggestive and emotionally powerful. He'd derived lasting faith in the power of omission in part by reading Rudyard Kipling, who dubbed nonessential words "the enemy of vigor." While Hemingway made plain that "a writer who omits things because he does not know them only makes hollow places in his writing," he emphasized that you can omit anything as long as you know what you've omitted. He believed an omission could "strengthen the story and make people feel something more than they understood."

In life, our capacity to feel outpaces our ability to understand, so the meaning we seek to impart in stories often revolves around their emotional effect. That may explain why a story can inspire empathy between even those who share dramatically different life philosophies. When you develop, it's essential that you remain focused on moving the reader and not on merely moving words around on the page.

When you develop, it's essential that you remain focused on moving the reader and not on merely moving words around on the page.

When we talk about development as a concept, we talk in the abstract, but the practice itself requires specific aims: You develop, for instance, to reduce the chance that the reader will guess the identity of the murderer before the true crime novel's resolution. You develop in order to raise the stakes and ratchet up the protagonist's inner conflict in a way that makes her more compelling and sympathetic. You develop to draw on additional sources that better explain the fundamentally different worldview governing late-nineteenth-century American immigrants, whose behavior would otherwise seem irrational.

In future chapters, we're going to share techniques that will help you pinpoint just which elements in your writing will benefit from development. In the meantime, for a valuable lesson in rewriting, search online or visit your local university archives and ask to see early drafts of great writers' work, then compare each draft to the published version. It's something that we all should do in school, if only to avoid the idea that the classics (or any completed work, for that matter) sprang fully formed from the brains of their creators, like the Greek goddess of wisdom, Athena, from Zeus's skull.

Or, in lieu of leaving your desk, imagine a flip book that conveys the reality of development: Fffffflip: sentences written, then unwritten, then written anew. Fffffflip: paragraphs that jump from one page to another or vanish altogether.

And you don't have to limit this exercise to text alone. Look closer: Ffffffflip: a character whose hair turns red, then brown, then black; who grows a mustache and acquires a gold earring; who dies and then comes back to life; who escapes with his sweetheart in a rowboat.

Flip through it forward or backward — you'll find a different version of the story unfolding in each case. Start from anywhere in the middle, and you'll find the beginnings of a third version. Start somewhere else, and you're on the verge of a fourth. Why not a fifth? *Now* you're developing.

SWEAT TRUMPS TALENT

> Experience has shown me that
> there are no miracles in writing.
> The only thing that produces good writing
> is hard work.

— ISAAC BASHEVIS SINGER

TWO BELIEFS ABOUT TALENT weigh heavily on the novice writer: first, that talent is an innate and mysterious gift that you either have or don't have and cannot develop; and second, that talent determines destiny. The dictionary seems to bolster these beliefs by declaring talent a "natural aptitude or skill." In the overall spirit of the Develop stage, let's adopt a more functional, dynamic definition: *Talent is a set of qualities that enable us to improve faster and rise to higher levels of achievement.*

According to this new definition, physical qualities like strength, flexibility, stamina, coordination, balance, rhythm, speed, and timing form the foundation for athletic talent. The qualities that make up writing talent aren't as clear-cut, since they involve more intellectual and psychological traits, including literacy (how much and what you read), imagination, analytical ability, tolerance for seclusion, patience, determination,

You've had to develop talent through sweat, the ability to work toward something over time.

and capacity for delayed gratification. No doubt you can think of others. When you were born, you were pure potential. Since then, whether you've chosen to write, play sports, or compose music, you've had to develop talent through sweat, the ability to work toward something over time.

The record books teem with athletes whom no one would initially have called talented but who prevailed anyway. Polio twisted Wilma Rudolph's left leg to the extent that she required a leg brace and special treatment until age twelve. Overjoyed to run and play like a normal kid, she resolved to become an athlete like her older sister. Eight years later, she overshot that goal, winning three world titles as a sprinter in the 1960 Rome Olympic Games.

A lesser-known athlete, Eric Courchesne had also suffered the effects of polio. He relied on crutches and braces to support his emaciated legs as he entered UC Berkeley's gymnastics room to train for the still rings event. Tall and lanky in the company of compact musclemen, he wouldn't have been mistaken for a guy with talent for the still rings, which require a soaring dismount and a solid landing. But Courchesne trained hard, crashing painfully to the mats hundreds of times because he couldn't bend his knees. Four years later, he landed a dismount with locked knees and became the powerhouse Pacific-8 Conference champion and one of the top still-rings performers in the United States.

We call Rudolph and Courchesne, as well as their nonathlete counterparts, role models because they serve as living testimony that sweat matters in ways most of us don't anticipate. Factors such as timing, circumstance, upbringing, culture of opportunity, and at least ten thousand hours of practice may contribute to success more than models like "talent" or "genuis," as Malcolm Gladwell suggests in *Outliers*. Even superstars rarely excel in all areas; most of us compensate for weakness in one area with strength in another. And we compensate for outright failure by refusing to quit.

> **Most of us compensate for weakness in one area with strength in another.**

The same logic applies to all fields. Albert Einstein credited his discoveries in physics to "curiosity and persistence." Fired from her first job, Oprah Winfrey rose above an abusive childhood and numerous other career setbacks. Walt Disney lost a job at the *Kansas City Star* because an editor said "he lacked imagination and had no good ideas." And Grand Ole Opry manager Jimmy Denny reportedly fired Elvis Presley after one performance and advised, "You ain't goin' nowhere, son. Go back to drivin' a truck." The high school yearbook staff rejected drawings submitted by Charles Schulz of *Peanuts* fame. In an essay years later, Schulz admirer Jonathan Franzen asked, "Was Charles Schulz's comic genius the product of his psychic wounds?"

When it comes to writing, we can develop our skills and boost our talent through thoughtful practice: we can augment our knowledge and perspective by reading books across genres, actively cultivating psychological traits such as empathy and sensitivity in the process, not to mention improving vocabulary and use of grammar and punctuation. By continuing to write, we build stamina and patience, eventually exceeding our standards to the extent that we can then raise them.

Perhaps most important of all, in the diligent application of our arts, we demonstrate our devotion to the work. Erica Jong observed, "Everyone has a talent, but rare is the courage to follow the talent to the places it leads." Caricaturist Al Hirschfeld said, "I believe that everybody is creative, and everybody is talented. I just don't think that everybody is disciplined. That is the rare commodity." Without discipline, we may fail to seek out or recognize opportunity, and without opportunity, what talent we possess means little. As Thomas Edison said, "Most people miss opportunity because it's dressed in overalls and looks like work." Development represents the supreme act of discipline because it not only looks like work; it *is* work.

Development not only looks like work; it *is* work.

Casual observers often mistake lack of experience for lack of talent. But the peers of accomplished athletes, painters, musicians, and writers know enough to recognize the perseverance that turned modest potential into high accomplishment, regardless of inauspicious beginnings. Failure in one arena may even serve as a necessary stepping-stone to success in another.

While no amount of effort can guarantee specific outcomes, sweat will reliably improve the odds that you'll achieve your goals, maybe even surpassing them to a degree that astonishes both you and your peers.

"But what about now?" you may ask. "Can something arise from what looks like nothing?" Of course — that's how the universe began.

DAN: THE CYCLES
AND LAYERS OF LEARNING

Character consists of what you do
on the third and fourth tries.

— JAMES MICHENER

EVERY BOOK PROJECT brings a unique writing experience, yet
more than a dozen of my works over the past few decades have
followed a cycle of psychological phases as consistent as those
of the moon. This eight-phase cycle describes my personal writing process, but I expect that many other writers will find one or
more phases familiar.

The cycle begins with what I call my *preprocrastination*
phase, when I know I'll be procrastinating soon but I'm not yet
ready to commit. This denial phase moves seamlessly into an
official *procrastination* period, when yard work and other projects take on an unexpected urgency. After decades of experience,
I no longer feel conflicted about not writing during this initial
part of the cycle. In fact, I respect and appreciate the beginning
of dream time as a necessary phase of percolation and subconscious preparation.

Then comes the *involved* phase, when I stretch, sit down

at the keyboard, and start typing. In the Dream stage, I'll jot down a few ideas or scene snippets, talk to myself aloud or on the page, make notes on initial research, and find relevant quotations I can use. Eventually, I'll make my way toward a What If question and partial outline. This phase of the cycle typically feels as if a huge locomotive is just beginning to chug, each car-coupling jarring against the next as the wheels slowly start turning and the engine within me strains to overcome inertia and build momentum, until it finally pulls out of the station. During this phase, I still take breaks at every opportunity.

Finally, ideas begin to flow as I enter the *interested* phase, when I'd rather be drafting than sharpening pencils or mowing the lawn. This phase lasts for days, weeks, or months, depending on the project, until I'm ready to shift gears again.

As I draft and develop, the interested phase alternates with the *immersion* phase of writing, as I enter a timeless zone in which the world recedes and becomes less real than the story or project. I forget about email and other business for hours that seem like minutes. This absorption becomes a feverish compulsion to keep pace with the creative flow. Uncounted pages flash by the locomotive's windows as the writing becomes a race through rising complications in the story world and in my own.

Once I sight a finish line on the horizon — the completion of a new draft — two short and intense periods follow each other: The *obsession* phase, in which I skip meals, ignore family, and couldn't care less what else is happening in the world. Then, in a final mad dash, the *desperation* phase culminates in an adrenalized all-nighter, and my own and my protagonist's adventures reach a simultaneous climax and resolution.

The cycle wouldn't be complete, however, without my

mentioning one other wild-card phase that intrudes at random — the *depression* phase, when, for whatever reason, I begin to view my work through a dark and distorted lens. *What was I thinking?* I wonder. *This is all crap.* There are occasions when depression provokes clear-eyed reflection. Sometimes it's necessary to scrap an ill-conceived project; I've done it more than once. But other times, I've managed to rescue mediocre early drafts with more layers of rigorous development — just as long as I still believe in the original dream.

I've managed to rescue mediocre early drafts with more layers of rigorous development.

Thus concludes a cycle that repeats itself not only with each book project and each layer of drafting but, to a lesser degree, with nearly every writing session. Progress unfolds in layers, each of which points to the next.

I relearned this lesson in the winter of 2006, on the eve of my sixtieth birthday, when I resolved to learn to ride a unicycle. A friend showed me the basics, after which, every morning for three weeks, alone on a double tennis court, I struggled, without any discernible progress, to stay atop that devilish wheel. In moments of dire need, I clung with one leather-clad hand to the chain-link fence surrounding the court as I strove mightily to stay balanced and moving.

The first day, it took me about an hour of starts and stops to make it all the way around the court. Every few feet, the unicycle would shoot out from under me, and I'd cling to the fence like a gecko before continuing. At the end of each practice session, I'd go for broke: pushing away from the fence, I leaned forward and, careening toward the center of the court, I counted how many pedals I could make before going down. I wasn't exactly riding yet — it was more like a delayed fall. By the end of the first week, my best count was six pedals before the uni and I parted ways.

During the second week, I noticed a group of women jogging past the courts each morning. One of them, presumably out of compassion, yelled, "You should really quit that!" And I did at the end of that day. Then I remembered a relevant quotation by psychologist and author David K. Reynolds, who said, "When running up a hill, it's okay to give up as many times as you like — as long as your feet keep moving." After another week back on the court, I managed eighteen pedals before my ride ended.

By the end of the third week, something had clicked: I could now ride figure eights. From atop the unicycle, I waved to the women as they jogged by. A small victory.

Learning to ride a unicycle reminded me that everything is difficult until it becomes easy — or at least easier. As Ralph Waldo Emerson put it, "Every artist was first an amateur." Over the course of the three weeks, there were several days when everything seemed to fall apart, but, nearly always, on the day following each so-called bad day, I experienced a breakthrough. It was precisely during each apparent regression that deep learning occurred. Persisting through the tough part made possible a quantum jump in progress. The pattern of crisis, setback, learning, and progress repeated itself in my gymnastics practice, relationships, and writing.

Persisting through the tough part made possible a quantum jump in progress.

I can't say I enjoy bad days, when my writing flounders, but I've come to accept these cycles and even to rely on them.

Another formative moment took place some years ago for both myself and my daughter and coauthor, Sierra. When she was four years old, Sierra liked to draw, as many children do, and I gave her a book called *Heidi's Horse*. The book contained Heidi's childhood drawings of horses, compiled by her mother over a ten-year time span. When Heidi was two, her drawings were mostly lines and squiggles, but by her third year, they resembled stick-figure horses, some with three or five legs. When I first presented Sierra with the book, I looked over her shoulder as she flipped it open to reveal a beautiful, shaded rendering of a horse, drawn by Heidi when she was twelve. Sierra gazed, wide-eyed, at this image and said, "I can't draw a horse like this."

"Well," I said, turning toward the beginning of the book, "let's see how Heidi drew horses when she was your age." When Sierra saw the drawings Heidi did at age four, her eyes brightened considerably. "That's just how I draw horses!" she exclaimed. Flipping through page by page, Sierra seemed to grasp, all at once, the idea of layers of learning and improvement over time. I left her immersed in the book.

When I looked in on her a little later, she was drawing horses.

YOUR MASTER METAPHOR

How we do anything
is how we do everything.

—— ZEN PROVERB

WHEN YOU DEVELOP YOUR WORK, you make the connection between what you write and how you live, because you want the one to meaningfully evoke the other. And when you crave inspiration, you can draw upon transformative experiences that we've come to call Master Metaphors.

At some point in your life, perhaps more than once, you achieved something, despite the odds against it, because of a longing or determination that you can't fully explain. It might be a skill that initially seemed out of reach or a one-time accomplishment: jumping off the high diving board, delivering a speech at a school assembly, or traveling to a distant country. That experience, as distinguished by the inexplicable feeling that accompanied it, forms your Master Metaphor. It's a barometer of your capacity to surpass limitations, even those that seem to define your character. Every Master Metaphor draws universal energy from particular life circumstances.

Before we can tell you how to identify your own Master Metaphor, it's important that you fully understand *metaphor* itself, because it's more than a literary term — it's the primary instrument by which story and life approach each other. As the Greek philosopher and teacher Aristotle says in his pioneering book on craft, *Poetics*: "The greatest thing by far is to have a command of metaphor.... It is the mark of genius. For to make good metaphors implies an eye for resemblances."

> **Your Master Metaphor is a barometer of your capacity to surpass limitations, even those that seem to define your character.**

Aristotle doesn't make a distinction between a true metaphor and a simile. The two both belong to the more general category of metaphorical or figurative language, though they have subtly different effects — for a good example, consider the lyrics to the 1968 song "The Windmills of Your Mind":

Like a clock whose hands are sweeping
Past the minutes of its face
And the world is like an apple
Whirling silently in space
Like the circles that you find
In the windmills of your mind.

In these lyrics, one simile follows the next (each beginning with "Like...") as they build up to the song's reigning metaphor: the windmills of your mind. It's a metaphor because the phrase equates two otherwise unrelated objects — and, above all, writers and storytellers seek truth by drawing connections.

In his *Poetics*, Aristotle also explains that he holds metaphors, and the ability to perceive them, in such high esteem because poetry arises from two distinct causes — man's instincts for imitation and for harmony and rhythm:

> [Man] is the most imitative of living creatures, and through imitation he learns his earliest lessons; and no less universal is the pleasure felt in things imitated.... Thus the reason why men enjoy seeing a likeness is that in contemplating it they find themselves learning or inferring, and saying perhaps "Ah, that is he."

In other words, we *have* to make those connections: we can describe ourselves and one another most fully only through associations and relations. When writers, artists, and innovators develop Aristotle's "eye for resemblances," we grasp the keystone to empathy in the essential unity of seemingly disparate experiences and objects (windmills, your mind) — and we also gain access to this powerful tool for our own advancement, the Master Metaphor.

Your Master Metaphor, above all, must bear deep meaning for you. It won't necessarily have any relation to creativity; it could be the labors exerted in order to ride a unicycle or learn to speak Arabic, but it doesn't need to lead to something highly visible or even hugely difficult in an objective sense. Even epic trials of heroes and gods are ultimately metaphors for the ordinary striving of men and women like ourselves. Master Metaphors are smaller, individual myths that speak to each of us in the privacy of our own minds.

In a memoir of his English school days, *Stand Before Your God*, novelist Paul Watkins describes becoming mindful of one such experience:

Once I dreamed that there was a dark-red river flowing just above my head. It was the river of untold stories. All I had to do was reach up and touch the river and the stories would pool like blood in my hands. I knew in my dream that it was a timeless river and easy to reach if you knew it was there. But that was the great secret. You had to know it existed.

I wrote it all down in the middle of the night, while a lightning storm burst so viciously overhead that it set off the fire alarms. As I wrote, I thought of the javelin that had sailed from my hand long ago at the Eagle House track meet and the angels that carried it up. I'd had the same feeling back then, that it was a strength I could use if only I knew how.

Master Metaphors derive their power from our awareness of them and our willingness to trust in them. In that remembered javelin throw, Watkins finds a symbol for his own ability to tap into what he elsewhere refers to as a "deep reservoir of strength," something at once within and beyond himself that also comes to orient him as a writer.

For those of us who pursue it seriously, writing may give rise to an especially keen Master Metaphor because it's an ongoing practice forcing us to move through so much that also afflicts us in life: fear, doubt, procrastination, feelings of emptiness, self-loathing, self-censorship, and paralysis. And we learn that it's not enough to conquer any of these foes just once — we may have to do so every writing session. The same troubles cycle around and around again, those whirling windmills of our psyches. Yet every time you stand up from a successful writing session — a period in which you've accomplished set goals — you'll have that much more evidence that you can do so again. That's the gift of a Master Metaphor: each accomplishment builds upon the past and forms a foundation for future endeavors.

Each accomplishment builds upon the past and forms a foundation for a future endeavor.

To identify your Master Metaphor, take up a new vantage point and look upon your life as though it were a constellation that you could behold only from afar. You may believe you've done so on previous occasions, when writing a résumé or a biographical text, but these activities have more to do with how you'd like to present yourself in accordance with the standards of a particular group or society at large. Your Master Metaphor will represent the triumph of your own potential set against your *own* standards.

When you search your memory, take the comparative weight of various experiences into account, not in terms of how much time they took or what position you achieved or even any sense of material reward, but as measured by their relative value to your life. In *Aspects of the Novel*, E. M. Forster pins down the contrast between time and value:

> There seems something else in life besides time, something which may conveniently be called "value," something which is measured not by minutes or hours, but by intensity so that when we look at our past it does not stretch back evenly but piles up into a few notable pinnacles, and when we look at the future it seems sometimes a wall, sometimes a cloud, sometimes a sun, but never a chronological chart.

And that peculiar intensity, the kind that colors a stead-fastness and tenacity that seem to have no cause — that's the glinting blade of a windmill that declares itself from the dim landscape of your past. You'll find your Master Metaphor amid those moments when you busted through the "walls" that Randy Pausch describes in *The Last Lecture*: "The brick walls are not there to keep us out; the brick walls are there to give us a chance to show how badly we want something."

In the film *Nurse Betty*, a bartender named Ellen gives the title character new direction in life when she shares her own Master Metaphor:

> Everybody told me not to go. But I wanted to go to Rome ever since I saw Audrey Hepburn in *Roman Holiday*, and goddammit, I went.... Rome was the best thing I ever did, because I DID IT! And I swear to you, it changed me. I've been to Rome, Italy! I sat every morning at the Café Sistina and had my cappuccino, and watched the pilgrims walk to mass, and no one can ever take that away from me.

As a writer seeking motivation or stamina, you may draw on your Master Metaphor during earlier stages, but you'll need it most when you develop, for this stage can bring deep uncertainty. At times, you won't be able to tell whether you're taking firmer hold of the dream or it's on the verge of slipping from your grasp.

This timeless memory — your Master Metaphor — tells you to write on, and to carry on, as you've done before, no matter the obstacles from within and without. It tells you that you've already developed too much to stop now. That there's no end except the end. Your Master Metaphor won't tell you precisely where to go, but it will tell you that you'll get there.

SIERRA: NEVER SURRENDER

Fate smashes us as though we were made of glass
And never are our shards put together again.

— ABU AL-ʿALAʾ AL-MAʾARRI

IN THE LATE SUMMER OF 2007, I found myself sweating in a
dark, dusty, and airless room precariously perched on a crum-
bling staircase at the very top of a traditional house in a strange
country. That country happened to be Syria. It was strange —
then — because I'd only arrived a few hours earlier. I'd come,
alone, for a language barely comprehensible after a year of
study, a language I had little reason to be learning besides an
unfathomable longing that would illuminate my late twenties
and my writing life.

When I'd first studied Arabic in Chicago, it had felt meaningful in the way of a promising new beginning, only the kind
that doesn't actually promise anything specific. I didn't even
realize just how much Arabic mattered to me until that dark first
night in Damascus, when, buoyed by the sensation of traveling,
I drew absurd comfort from the conviction that I would endure
real discomfort if necessary. *Why so necessary?* I might easily
have asked myself. I didn't know then that studying Arabic

would give rise to a Master Metaphor, that it would lastingly expand my sense of what I might be and do.

Previously, during several months in Cairo and my first plunge into the world of spoken Arabic, I'd practiced Egyptian dialect at a small, extraordinarily cheap private academy while interning with the Associated Press. After completing journalism school, I moved to Washington, DC, to write about higher education. Yet I found myself working my way through a stack of language textbooks in the early mornings, during my lunch breaks, and in the evenings. It made little sense, but I rarely thought it through. Occasionally I felt like Wile E. Coyote in pursuit of the Road Runner — in leaving Cairo, I'd run right off the cliff, so when would I fall down? Over seven years and counting I've kept on running — reading and speaking a language I chose for myself — and I haven't fallen yet. Studying Arabic helped me keep on writing, because it showed me that you have to leave the road and run out into thin air, that there's no other way.

But let's go back: Before I attempted Arabic, I didn't think of myself as having any particular talent for languages. I'd forgotten far more than I remembered of four previous tongues. I'd also written thousands of pages before I moved overseas, most of them for assignments that didn't instill in me any real confidence that I might write for my own reasons and not someone else's. Arabic would teach me that certain kinds of desire can only justify themselves after the fact, if indeed they ever need to do so.

In the meantime, a few months after I briefly returned to the Middle East for that sojourn in Syria, I bought a one-way ticket to Lebanon and rented a room in its capital city, Beirut, an explosively vital seaside fantasia that famously never surrenders.

Like every ancient city, it peddles contradictions. I lived in the urban equivalent of a marble maze, but a ten-minute walk down California Street would find me leaning over the corniche railing, the Mediterranean breeze stroking my face. Roaming the streets, I soon discovered that I could turn anyone — cab drivers, waiters, street vendors, artists — into an Arabic teacher, in much the same way that I had learned to cultivate a writing guide in every book. The world became my classroom, and ordinary life took on the luster of the extraordinary because every experience simultaneously advanced plot, revealed character, and conveyed important information about the culture that enveloped me.

The world became my classroom, and ordinary life took on the luster of the extraordinary.

As Adam Gopnik has written, "You breathe in your first language; you swim in your second." Arabic made it possible for me to breathe underwater, and it was a surreal experience. I taught my expatriate-raised Lebanese boyfriend the Arabic letters by pinning them to construction paper cutouts of feet and pasting them to his wall. "Just keep trying no matter what," those feet seemed to say as they made steady progress upward, "and the impossible will become ordinary." Learning Arabic, living in and writing about Beirut, not to mention writing well, often felt impossible, which made it all the more satisfying when I arrived at any real progress. Without the possibility of failure, success has little meaning; when failure becomes downright probable, even a small success comes to resemble the joyful end to a Hollywood movie, Jimmy Stewart in *It's a Wonderful Life*, running through the streets and gleefully exclaiming, "My mouth's bleeding!" to bemused passersby.

While living in Lebanon, I explored the country and read

about it, and I wrote radio stories, magazine articles, and a book profiling Lebanese artists. The work set me moving back and forth between the real city and the invented one, the present and the past, my own small life and dramatic events all the more contingent on it because I worked as a journalist — and because I paid attention.

Months passed, then several years. I had gradually become what I call an insider-outsider, simultaneously floating inside the unfolding story of a country not my own, yet able, with some effort, to step outside of the narrative and gain insight into it, a writer's insight, not that of a political scientist. I looked back at both the United States and my own past as though from outer space. The French poet Paul Éluard wrote, "There are other worlds, and they are in this one." Some of those worlds you can reach by plane or train; others lie within. Beirut turned out to be, for me, one of those crossroads where the inner and the outer journeys meet.

I'd never expected to feel entirely comfortable in Lebanon, and my lack of expectation made me perversely comfortable. That paradox led me to conclude that writing should be a struggle, that pain and pleasure are inexorably bound up with each other, and that the one must be present so the other can serve as its respite. I'd witnessed and experienced a degree of suffering before I moved overseas, but as an insider-outsider, I recognized in Beirut both the embodiment and the subversion of the suffering artist: the artist never seeks to increase her own suffering, but she won't let it block her from creating the art that can liberate her in mind and spirit, if not in body.

Because I suffered in order to learn Arabic — at the most extreme, long exposure to water pollution caused my hair to begin falling out — I knew the weight of it in my own life, and

I followed that weight like a plumb line down and down and discovered that my own desire could be depthless, that when it came to what really moved me, what meant the world to me, I too would not surrender.

> When it came to what really moved me, what meant the world to me, I too would not surrender.

And one day, when I eventually sat down to write a story that no one had assigned me, something felt different. I knew it might still be impossible, that I could hardly become impervious to doubt or terror or others' judgment. But such knowledge felt far away and irrelevant. It sailed over me like the planes that had once passed through the corner of my balcony window in that rented room where I wrote my first book. Just before I began that story, I'd gone on television to present the book, speaking in and understanding the Arabic talk-show chitchat — as unexpected a milestone to me as walking on the moon.

Now it seems obvious: it's the connections that matter most, not the substance of our accomplishments but rather the faith and commitment that rise up in response to desire's call. In the end, each of us can only recognize our true selves from the back because we're finally headed in the right direction. North, south, east, west? Who knows. As long as it's away from where we started.

OBJECTIVE: FOLLOW
THE GOLDEN THREAD

We have only to follow the thread of the hero path, and...
where we had thought to slay another we shall slay ourselves.
Where we had thought to travel outward,
we shall come to the center of our own existence.

— JOSEPH CAMPBELL

THE SAME GOLDEN THREAD that serves the developing story-teller first enabled the Athenian hero Theseus to make his way back to the mouth of the labyrinth after reaching its heart and slaying the Minotaur, a man with the head of a bull. In this myth and in any story, the golden thread defines the most immediate route between the beginning and the end of the hero's and the writer's journeys. Ariadne, the daughter of the Athenians' enemy, King Minos, broke ranks with her father and gave Theseus the ball of thread and a sword for the oldest reason in the world: she fell in love with him. And the story ultimately made possible by that love forms a metaphor for the Develop stage.

It's not difficult to identify Ariadne as Theseus's muse or to recognize in the Minotaur all that threatens to distract and obstruct you from telling the story you've by now resolved to tell. In order to prevail, you must enter the labyrinth, your draft awaiting development; overcome your own Minotaur with the help of the muse; and then find and follow your golden thread to an ending that mirrors and amplifies a beginning in a story that fuses your dream with the reader's.

This ancient myth has yet more to teach us. First, it's worth noting that the killing of the Minotaur comes too early in the story to form its climax; indeed, the outcome of this combat has no meaning until Theseus successfully escapes the labyrinth by way of the golden thread. It's not enough, in other words, for us to devote ourselves wholly to surpassing obstacles — we need to set our sights on higher creative goals, indicated but not yet achieved by our drafts. That's development.

We need to set our sights on higher creative goals, indicated but not yet achieved by our drafts.

Myth enables us to talk about all these elements of storytelling in abstract terms, but when it comes to each of us, and to each story, the terms couldn't be more concrete. You find and follow a story's golden thread by reviewing your layers of text and, as necessary, other supporting documents, such as your What If, dialogues, mind maps, and outlines — and asking yourself, not merely *Is this any good?* but rather *Does it belong to this story?* and *Could this story endure and thrive without it?* Not just the story as a whole but each page, paragraph, and sentence must anchor a coherent series of resonant ideas that come together into one whole and that connect with the reader.

The golden thread offers Theseus a single route out of the maze, and he must take that route in order to free himself. Likewise, you need to turn away from the labyrinth of infinite possibilities from which any story emerges and to speed toward that Platonic Ideal, the story's one true form, in which each turning point compels the one following it in an unexpected yet satisfying way.

And don't confuse the golden thread with your story's bare-bones central plotline — that collision between the protagonist's desire or will with one or more obstacles. Unique to each story, the golden thread defines not just what happens but *why* it happens. For that reason, branching subplots should meaningfully support the central plot, reveal character, intensify theme and emotion, and relay information that the reader needs in order to understand the overall story, what's known as exposition.

It's about making the story work on multiple, interrelated levels. As playwright Edward Albee once put it in a master class, "The difference between something that works and something that fails is — something that fails is arbitrary, something that works is inevitable." Even if we can also recognize some sense of illusion in that inevitability, we nonetheless come face to face with it every time we pick up our favorite books — would we truly want them to play out any other way? No, not even the tragedies, as Milan Kundera explains in *The Unbearable Lightness of Being* when he comments on the title character of Tolstoy's *Anna Karenina*:

> [Human lives] are composed like music. Guided by his sense of beauty, an individual transforms a fortuitous occurrence (Beethoven's music, death under a train) into a motif, which then assumes a permanent place in the composition of the individual's life. Anna could have chosen another way to take her life. But the motif of death and the railway station, unforgettably bound

to the birth of love, enticed her in her hour of despair with its dark beauty. Without realizing it, the individual composes his life according to the laws of beauty even in times of greatest distress.

The Brazilian architect Oscar Niemeyer made the same point in fewer words when he said, "Form follows beauty." It's *that* beauty toward which the golden thread always flows: the story's meaningful beauty. One important caveat: inevitability doesn't mean that authors couldn't have made different choices; it means that they fully justified the choices they did make.

In preparing yourself to follow your own golden thread, you'll confront two different kinds of obstruction: your doubts and your enthusiasm. You've had plenty of time to acquaint yourself with doubt during the Dream and Draft stages, which makes it all the more essential that you guard against the second liability — a stubborn, creative greed so fittingly captured in the figure of that bull-headed man. When you develop, an impulse may seize you much like that which overwhelms the traveler packing at the last moment: you may think, *Why, I might need absolutely anything, and everything, during the days ahead!* But your suitcase, at least, possesses a definite shape and volume, a material limitation on what it can accommodate. Your story may seem a different sort of vessel, potentially boundless. So why shouldn't you pack into it everything you've ever seen, felt, known, and loved? Isn't the purpose of story to express who you are in all your dazzling particularity? What could be more meaningful than that?

Your story will capture something of who you are — but only if you cling to that golden thread by embracing just those ideas and descriptions, those events and characters, that inevitably belong to the story. To do otherwise is to condemn yourself to wandering the labyrinth forever, mesmerized by all the possible alternative courses of action, committing to none, unable or unwilling to make the choices without which there is no story.

Cling to that golden thread by embracing just those ideas and descriptions that inevitably belong to the story.

Your sense of a story's golden thread will enable you to make the difficult cuts that development may require. Mary Karr had already written two successful memoirs, but that didn't make developing her third, *Lit*, any easier. "I threw this book away twice," she has said, by which she means that she trashed more than 1,000 pages, at one point salvaging only about 120 pages, mere months before her publication deadline:

> I walked around in my bathrobe for three days and made obscene gestures at the rafters. And there are a couple of people I call at such times, sort of the way the president would push the red button. I'd call these people. So I called Don DeLillo, and DeLillo sends me a postcard that says "write or die." I think I sent him one back that said "write *and* die."

It takes courage to let go of your own work, but Karr put her faith in the story, not merely in the existing text; eventually, she too found her golden thread, her way out of the maze of confusion and despair.

Before we conclude, let's return briefly to the story of Theseus and Ariadne: It ends happily at first. But they eventually part, and Ariadne weds Dionysus, the god of ritual madness.

Like Theseus, we too must eventually say farewell to the muse. When we dream and draft, we open up like flowers in spring, but then we begin to contract around our own stories. When we develop, we accept that knowing the way will mean going that way because it's the only way — because it has to be.

ALLEGIANCE TO STORY

> First I write the screenplay.
> Then I add in the dialogue.
>
> — ALFRED HITCHCOCK

IN THIS CHAPTER, we aim to help you approach your manuscript as an early reader might, so that you may gain insight into how to transform it as a writer. In *The Art of Fiction*, John Gardner says, "The writer is more servant than master of his story." Now you know it, and your labors at this stage prove it.

During development, you need to remind yourself that you owe your primary allegiance to the essence of your story and that your manuscript may have deviated from it — either in a material way or because it doesn't yet convey the emotional experience you intend. As you review each new layer, ask yourself, *Does this draft convey to readers the full story that I want to tell?* It's the essential question at this stage, and answering it will require you to clearly distinguish between the movie in your mind and what's actually transmitted by the written version, even as you've already spent days, weeks, or months striving to integrate the two.

In working to determine what kind of gap, if any, remains between your story and your manuscript, and how to close it, you can draw upon two analytical exercises — and you should do so to whatever degree that they illuminate new possibilities and motivate you to keep working.

Cultivate the distance you now need in order to assess what you have and haven't achieved on paper.

In the first exercise, which we'll call a *story check*, you'll compare a story summary with a bare-bones plot outline. First, set aside your current draft. Write a short synopsis — no more than one to three pages for a long-form work — of the intrinsic story you *want* to tell. This synopsis should highlight major characters, important turning points, and the emotional landscape that you're working to evoke. Consult, as necessary, your What If and earlier notes but not your manuscript. We're suggesting you create this synopsis in the Develop stage, as opposed to earlier, because you're doing so with a stage-specific purpose: to cultivate the distance you now need in order to assess what you have and haven't achieved on paper.

Next, you'll want to work from your latest draft to create a plot outline. Any outlining you did previously served a different function altogether: it organized your thoughts and ideas so that you might translate them into narrative. When you outline in the Develop stage, you do the reverse, translating what's expressed in sentences and paragraphs into an ordered list of events that omits description and dialogue and focuses on answering one question: *In each successive moment of your story, what actually happens?* Put down every event, in order, from first to last.

If your plot is complex, your cast of characters large, or your story nonlinear, then you may prefer a less linear and more associative model or diagram, like a mind map. Additionally, if you're more visual or tactile, you can storyboard as screenwriters do, constructing, rather than composing, your outline from index cards or Post-it notes, attaching them to a poster board or a wall, or dealing them out onto the floor of a large room. In whatever form you choose to work, the principle remains the same: you're constructing a record of the events in your story.

When your plot outline is complete, you'll be ready to perform the two interlocking tasks that form the mortar and pestle of development: First, review your outline point by point and appraise the extent to which it — and, by extension, your current draft — adheres to the story represented by your synopsis. You can start with the following questions:

❖ On the most basic level, are the events in your plot outline consistent with your story as described in the synopsis?

❖ Do events described in the synopsis play out in the same way in your plot outline?

❖ Do the climactic turning points represented in your synopsis appear as such in your plot outline — or are they getting lost in a sea of competing events?

❖ If you were to draw a line to graph the emotional affect these plot points convey, what would it look like?

❖ How does this graph compare with your original intentions as represented in your synopsis?

❖ Do your intentions need to change? Or your manuscript?

Like a compass, this comparison of synopsis and outline may point your revisions in a new direction. Alternatively, if you're still too close to your manuscript to see distinctions between what you've written and the story you want to tell, you could ask a friend or hire someone else, such as a freelance editor, to draw up the plot outline and do the analysis — you'll still need to create the synopsis as a guide. At the least, such an outside appraisal may serve as a rewarding check on your own instincts.

As you continue this exercise, turn your attention to the story itself as expressed by the synopsis and again take a reader's perspective: Do you find what happens convincing? Satisfying? Now comes a pivotal question: *Is the story that you're struggling to write the one that you'd actually want to read?* Be honest with yourself. If the answer is "no" or "possibly not," then you'll need to understand why before you can move forward. You may only now realize definitively that challenges you experienced while drafting pointed to flaws in the original story concept.

We've all been there, and there's a remedy: Your manuscript, due to length or complexity, will probably seem less amenable to change. But you pledge your allegiance to your story, in part, because it remains mutable — and the synopsis aims to make it more accessible. You can rework the synopsis as necessary and then draw up a plan to produce a revised draft. Just take it one step at a time — and then you'll know that you're actually moving forward and not just marching in place.

> **Your story remains mutable. You can rework the synopsis as necessary and then draw up a plan to produce a revised draft.**

As you undertake the preceding exercise, you're driving toward another significant question, this one about the manuscript itself: *What story does the reader take from the existing draft?* To answer that, another layer of analysis may prove ideal for shorter pieces, and time-consuming yet rewarding for longer works. In this second exercise, you'll construct what might be called a *reader discovery outline*, compiled from the answers to one question: *At each successive moment of this story, what does the reader know?*

You're no longer limiting yourself to plot points alone — this layer of analysis also encompasses character biography and details of story world and setting. Go through your manuscript page by page, paragraph by paragraph, even line by line if your work's particularly complex. As you do, take notes in the margins of the text, or on a separate page, as to exactly what information the text relays to the reader.

Keep your intention in mind: you're not trying to compile an encyclopedia based on your own work; you're checking that readers know precisely *what* they need to know *when* they need to know it. You're assessing your own use of exposition — factual information that must be subtly incorporated into plot, description, and dialogue, and without which your readers can't fully appreciate the story.

As you undertake these exercises and other, more free-form assessments that direct new revisions and make the Develop stage as analytical as it is imaginative, craft takes on its single greatest importance in the five stages. By *craft*, we mean every useful (or at least useful-sounding) word of wisdom, or principle, or technique as to plot, character, story world, setting, theme, and to some extent language — it's time to bring them out one by one, as lenses through which you'll reexamine your manuscript.

How? Turn observations and axioms into questions that you can answer. And be as specific as possible. Vague queries like, *Is my plot strong?* won't help. Novelist Justin Kramon, for instance, has defined plot as "the intersection of what happens with what you're expecting to happen," an observation that yields a number of other questions you can ask yourself:

- ❖ What might I expect to happen at a given moment?
- ❖ What does then happen?
- ❖ What effect does the intersection of the two likely have on the reader?
- ❖ Could the two intersect in a more satisfying way that would heighten suspense? Or reveal character? Or move the reader?

The axiom "Show, don't tell" also conceals more precise questions, such as:

- ❖ I've summarized a year's occurrences in two paragraphs. Might any of these events deserve a scene of its own?
- ❖ Of the existing scenes, does each contribute anything to the reader beyond the information it articulates?
- ❖ Might that information be presented more efficiently?

It's worth pointing out that experienced writers understand "Show, don't tell" as shorthand expressing the difference between dramatic scene and summary narration. For instance, in a novel about a marriage, a three-page scene might cover the couple's argument from beginning to end, beat by beat, whereas only four paragraphs may be necessary to describe the thirteen years that follow their divorce, leading up to another scene in which the couple meets again for the first time. In other words, "show" and "tell" each serve different purposes — and both are useful to the extent that they serve the story.

Not sure what works best for you? Experiment. Find out.

You could conceivably spend hours or days on the preceding exercises. It's up to you whether to prepare a detailed assessment and then plunge into rewriting or to rewrite as you go.

Not sure what works best for you? Experiment. Find out. Ultimately, these exercises aim to unite the writer and the reader within each of us: the agent who acts and also the observer who's capable of stepping back and making the most of a capacity for self-observation. We all move back and forth between living and watching ourselves live, between creating and wondering at what we've created. It's our creations that draw these two viewpoints into alignment like patterns seen in the night sky, constellations that may stand in for eyes looking down on us as our stories unfold.

YOUR VOICE, YOUR PERSONA

> You have to write many words
> before you find your voice as a writer.
>
> — HENRY MILLER

YOU WON'T DISCOVER your writing voice as you might find a lost wallet on the sidewalk. You'll develop both your own voice, sometimes also called a *persona*, and individual voices for your characters in the same way you may once have developed your own style of handwriting, whether consciously or unconsciously — through use and in layers.

The comparison with handwriting has value because we're less likely to question the need to practice how we form words in order to do so more clearly and elegantly. When the young German poet Rainer Maria Rilke met author Lou Andreas-Salomé, the older woman who would transform his life and his art, he not only adopted the name Rainer on her suggestion but also altered his script to model hers. Rilke's handwriting bears another message: even those attributes for which we may become known as writers, we adopt or adapt from others. Keep the words of Ecclesiastes in mind: "What has been will be again, what has been done will be done again; there is nothing new under the sun." It's the particular way in which we bring together our innovations on imitation that makes a mark.

Voice, in this context, refers most generally to the way a text, whether fiction or fact, sounds as though it were spoken by one person — not necessarily an immediately identifiable person but a discrete individual nonetheless. Then again, some writers' voices are influential enough to inspire entire schools of imitators, such as Ernest Hemingway, so easily parodied: "Why did the chicken cross the road? To die. In the rain." But Hemingway too (as we discussed in an earlier chapter) had to develop the concise style that we associate so closely with his voice.

In mechanical terms, voice ultimately comes down to choice. A handful of elements contribute to what we perceive as the writer's voice on paper or in performance, such as distinctive vocabulary, idiom, and sentence structure, as well as overall story structure and variations in emotional tone and pacing. If it's not distinctive, then it's not voice. In the end, however, there are only so many elements, so, once more, it's the particular combination of elements that distinguishes one writer's voice from another's.

It's the particular combination of elements that distinguishes one writer's voice from another's.

Your voice on the page also reflects your environment and what you read. A books' primary function is to translate speech into text, and what you read influences how you speak, and so on. When we say a text has "voice," it may simply be a way of declaring the translation successful, indicating that you've found a way to compensate for the loss of body language, musicality, and direct control of tone and pace. The more you actively play with language, modifying your own usages so as to produce different effects on and off the page, the more you see just how it's possible to develop what previously may have seemed immutable — even as you'll do so gradually over hundreds and then thousands of pages.

> **It's possible to develop what previously may have seemed immutable.**

It's worth noting, however, that voice can become a collaborative affair. Writers in translation, for instance, arguably possess a different voice in each language; despite the translator's best effort to adhere to the original, the final text will speak with more than one tongue. The voice that you associate with any given author also owes something to the editorial process. In one particularly extreme example, what you might identify as Raymond Carver's voice actually emerged from collaboration between Carver and his editor, Gordon Lish.

When Carver sent Lish the manuscript of his soon-to-be-famed short-story collection *What We Talk About When We Talk About Love*, Lish radically altered it, effacing about half of the text, pruning more than that from three stories, and rewriting the endings of fourteen. According to Giles Harvey, writing in the *New York Review of Books*, Lish rescued a "leaner, quieter, more agile book" from an original text that was "dense with sentimentality and melodrama." As readers, we register the author's name on the cover and conclude that stories emerge from a single voice. As writers, we come to know better.

With the help of our editors, we need to eliminate those idiosyncrasies that do not constitute voice — which must serve story — but rather diminish its power, such as the frequent use of interjections like *indeed* or *well* or repetitive use of modifiers like *totally* or *very*. These eccentricities of language may form a charming aspect of the writer's speaking voice in real life, an arena that tolerates far more diversity. When the author speaks on the page to readers, in contrast, he speaks through an edited version of his real self, the *persona*.

By taking the term *persona* as a lens through which to view both a writer's voice and the voices of her characters, you can recognize points of connection that enable you to develop both. When considering your own voice, your own character on the page, you can assume the vantage point from which you approach each of your characters' individual voices in dialogue and interior monologue. You can also see the way individual points of view interact to form a story. The same principles that make dialogue effective and memorable also apply to the story in its entirety because as you tell the story or spin out an idea, it becomes a dialogue with the reader — one in which you may speak in many voices.

In the previous chapter, you assessed your manuscript from a reader's perspective, but you can make it more authentic and convincing by also reviewing it through the eyes of your characters. A blink-and-you'll-miss-it scene in the film *Shakespeare in Love* encapsulates an essential truth about story: A serving wench asks the actor who plays the nurse in an Elizabethan production of *Romeo and Juliet* just what the play is about. He replies, "It's about this nurse..." Consider the difference between the spectators' perspectives ("It's about two star-crossed lovers...") and the perspectives of individual characters (such as the nurse), who are naturally inclined to see the story in terms of their own lives and act accordingly.

Here you can perform another exercise, one complementary to the two discussed in the previous chapter. When writing story, whether fiction or creative nonfiction, take each character's point of view as your own, and review your text, scene by scene, asking on the character's behalf the key questions that actors are trained to ask: *What do I (as this character) want? What's in my way? What do I do to get what I want?* Together these questions help answer a larger one: *Who am I?* Asking the first three questions enables you to answer the fourth in a way that is *specific*, *believable*, and *compelling* — they're pillars of craft. When you evaluate each character's choices and actions, you can ask: Is this choice specific? Is it believable? Is it compelling? To make the most of that last question, break it down: Is the choice or action motivated? Whom does it affect? How? How high are the stakes? Actors must compensate for weaknesses in their answers, dictated by the text, but if writers don't like the answers, they can change the text.

> You're giving voice to what truly matters to you, what defines you.

The stories you choose to tell and the characters you champion will play a role in shaping your voice. You're giving voice to what truly matters to you, what defines you, or at least who you believe yourself to be. In our real lives, over time, each of us adopts a voice to suit the persona that has emerged from choice and chance. It's all part of those conversations we're continually having with ourselves, only now more consciously — an endless loop of talking and listening, of takes and retakes, of developing ourselves as we develop our work, so that each of us can finally conclude, *Ah*, that's *me*.

QUESTIONS:
HELP US HELP YOU

Advice is what we ask for
when we already know the answer,
but wish we didn't.

— ERICA JONG

A WRITTEN WORK doubles as a room into which we invite others when we ask for their feedback. Ideally, that room will attract a convivial crowd, maybe even generate a line out the door. We secretly fear that a mere handful of people will wander in, only to make an abrupt about-face when they encounter what's there — we may want to flee on their heels.

The less invested *you* are in that room, in that demanding stack of pages, the more likely you are to want to abandon it without even looking back. That makes it all the more important that you choose an appropriate time to throw open your doors or even to quietly usher in a single guest with one finger to your lips.

The Develop stage marks such a moment. Astute feedback will reduce time away between rounds of editing and renew your sense of purpose.

To that end, we've devised a list of questions that we recommend you ask yourself, as well as fellow writers and potential readers. We intend these questions to help you assess your readiness to digest feedback and to clarify just what kind of counsel you seek at any particular moment. You'll also be better equipped to choose those readers most likely to give you what you need when you need it — as the saying goes, we're all one another's angels and demons.

Questions for Yourself

1. *What kind of feedback will best help you develop your manuscript?* There are two primary reasons to seek feedback in the Develop stage: Actual readers' feelings about your latest draft may recalibrate your instincts, revealing weaknesses and possibilities in your manuscript that you hadn't previously glimpsed. Alternatively, you may simply want one or more witnesses to what you've produced so far, who can also motivate you to keep working. In that case, there's nothing wrong with directly requesting encouragement and taking care to approach those people most able to give it.

2. *Can you formulate questions about your own manuscript?* The more exact your questions, the more effective they become. For instance, the question "Is my plot intriguing?" may yield only a yes or no — the first reassuring, the second alarming, but neither particularly useful

to revision. Be more specific: "When character X decides to do action Y with character Z, did you find it believable? Did it move you? Did you wish for or expect something else to happen?"

3. *Is your allegiance to your story itself or only to the current incarnation of it?* As you read through your current draft, maintain awareness of the story behind it, as though you were peering through the slats in a picket fence to a garden scene beyond. Ask yourself whether you'd be willing to cut blocks of text or reorder them or dramatically alter the language. If you feel a strong resistance to making any changes, you probably won't recognize even excellent feedback as such. Revisit older drafts, because nothing will better persuade you of the value of more edits than the benefit to your manuscript of those you've already made.

4. *How strong a connection have you cultivated with your story?* Sometimes when we ask for feedback, we're actually asking for permission to lay aside the work. That permission, if granted by our readers, may ease our way in transitioning to new, more meaningful projects. Or we may be capitulating to self-doubt. How to know the difference? Keep working on the project, but make time to explore others as well — one of them may eventually justify or even demand a shift of allegiance. At the least, writing onward will enable you to develop courage and stamina.

Questions for Fellow Writers

1. *When do you first ask for feedback, and why?* Every writer's answer will differ to some degree, and for each work, but discussions on the subject will reveal much about how fellow writers think about writing, especially if they're more experienced. We all learn through trial and error, but there's no reason you have to commit every error yourself. Then again, keep in mind that someone else's error could also turn out to be the right choice for you.

2. *What types of feedback do you find most valuable, and what strategies have you found effective in soliciting useful feedback?* In service to your story, you need to assess the value of feedback, not merely react emotionally to it — but take more seriously any advice that provokes an intense emotional reaction. Hearing about others' experiences dealing with feedback will change your frame of reference, console you, and help you develop your own process for requesting, absorbing, and applying readers' comments.

3. *How did feedback influence you to edit specific past works?* It's not always easy to know how to apply even just one suggestion: Accept it? Reject it? There are other alternatives, and the comments of fellow writers can shed light on them. Comrades will always play a significant role in the journey that manuscripts take from inspiration to publication. Stories by other writers

about dramatic changes to their own manuscripts help liberate yours from the straitjacket of isolated authorship. Remember: we write alone, together.

4.   *Do your first readers want to read more of your work? What do you do to encourage that kind of loyalty?* It's important that, as storytellers, we build a community from which our works will emerge. In *The Secret Miracle: The Novelist's Handbook*, Jennifer Egan says, "[My readers] need to be on my side — i.e. wanting me to write a good book, rather than a bad book.... When I find someone who is a helpful and willing reader, I really try to hold onto them." Readers willing to review multiple works demonstrate a confidence in your ability as a storyteller that is powerfully motivating. However, you may need to remind your readers that they owe their primary allegiance to the particular story they're evaluating and not to your hopes or feelings. You'll need at least a few readers who can maintain the necessary distance from you; your friends will quite literally hear your voice when they read your stories, while your readers mostly won't. When you exchange work with fellow writers, you'll gain additional perspective, and your own ability to give and receive feedback will develop with time. You can begin a discussion about what works for each of you and share insight with one another.

Questions to Help You Choose Readers

1. *Have you previously given feedback on works in progress?*
   All readers have opinions; only some can articulate
   them in a way that will help you develop and refine your
   manuscript.

2. *When you're discussing books or movies, for instance, with
   friends, do you find it challenging to disagree with them?* The
   reader who's uncomfortable telling you that he didn't
   like the movie you love will probably find it difficult to
   negatively critique your manuscript. The kind of distance
   that separates people who are afraid to disagree with
   each other isn't the kind of distance you're looking for.

3. *If you don't like a work, are you more likely just to turn
   away from it, or do you find yourself mulling over why you
   didn't like it?* Reading itself need not be an analytical
   process, but critiquing requires that kind of impulse. It's
   best to approach those people already naturally inclined
   to wonder, because curiosity is not an inclination that
   gushes up abruptly like an oil well.

4. *Can you find time to read my work and comment on it? How
   soon?* Practical questions like these make a difference.
   Settle on a time frame at or before the point when you
   hand off your manuscript. The person who takes your
   work and holds on to it for a year will create a discour-
   aging uncertainty best avoided. Don't forget to reward

readers who offer valuable critiques within the agreed-upon time period.

5. *After one initial round of feedback, would you be willing and able to discuss the work further and/or read later drafts?* Your readers won't always respond honestly, so you need to develop alternate strategies to gauge their sincerity. For instance, readers who express enthusiasm to read multiple drafts, then offer mainly positive feedback but decline to review later drafts — well, their actions may say more than their words.

6. *How important is it to you that I apply your feedback?* It may disconcert some readers if you fail to implement some or any of their suggestions. Feedback that initially strikes you as reasonable could later prove unworkable. In that case, you may need to seek out alternate readers. Be up-front with your readers about how you write — you'll be less likely to offend them later on, and talking about your own process will help you better understand it.

We've included queries throughout the text because it's important that you not only ask questions but also train yourself to ask the right questions at the right time. Even when you find answers, learn to recognize them for what they truly are — the beginning of new questions. It's something we do naturally, whenever we're making progress.

WHEN THE WORLD BECOMES
YOUR TEACHER

I am pretty sure that writing may be
a way of life in itself.
It can be that because
it continually forces us
away from self toward others.

— MADELEINE L'ENGLE

THE MORE YOU IMMERSE YOURSELF in your story, the more adept you'll become at shaping the narrative on the page, but only to the extent that you also allow the story to shape the way you see the world. As it turns out, it's not enough to develop your story, because the strength of what you express on the page, no matter the subject, will ultimately rest on how much *you* develop in the telling.

In order to understand why, it's helpful to contemplate the difference between a picture window and a porthole. When you look through a picture window, you enjoy the illusion that you can see everything there is to see — and it's a comforting illusion. Stories, however, offer us no such illusion. They better resemble portholes that frame a scene and direct readers' attention toward a particular view, a moment of transformation.

Look at this, they say. Look at it closely because it matters, even if it's not all that matters.

As Susan Sontag's novel *In America* begins, an unnamed narrator, present only in the opening chapter, approaches her own picture window, one that looks out on late-nineteenth-century Poland: "Irresolute, no, shivering, I'd crashed a party in the private dining room of a hotel." At that party, the narrator quickly singles out a woman who herself seizes the attention of others, the kind of woman around whom an enthralling story might emerge like an appropriately wild terrain around a lioness and her pride: "When she moved about the room, she was always surrounded; when she spoke, she was always listened to."

Sontag's narrator makes one last choice before disappearing into the text: she follows this remarkable woman "out into the world." Just like this narrator, an association surely not lost on Sontag, we writers single out characters or ideas worth following and give ourselves up to them. If we do our work well, our readers too will share in the sense of promise that defines great stories. It's why all of us read — because we seek something, anything, that stands a chance of changing everything for the better. Even if only for one golden moment.

We writers single out characters or ideas worth following and give ourselves up to them.

When you set out to tell a story, you begin by looking at the world through a picture window. When you dream and draft, you select elements of that view around which you'll frame a porthole, one that — as you develop — increasingly encompasses what inevitably belongs to the story and excludes what doesn't. As the porthole of your story begins to come together, however, it may also become something that you can take out into the world, like a large and invisible monocle, one that performs an unusual task: it directs your attention to the objects, people, landscapes, and events that relate in some way to your unfolding story — just as long as you pay attention.

Sometimes the connections will be literal and concrete: You may find a resting place in your manuscript for the scarab paperweight you noticed on a real-life acquaintance's desk. The disarming gesture of a stranger, half-vulnerable and half-smug, might grant you abrupt insight into a real-life character's psyche. Or the way the moon seems to rest on the slope of a hillside like a child's head on her mother's shoulder may complete a fictional scene in which your protagonist decides to go home after a long absence.

Other times, this new perspective on the world better resembles a feeling, a glimpse of *time outside of time* — either the intensely focused rapture of lovers or the transcendent state that psychotherapist and author Irvin D. Yalom refers to as "an ontological state (a state of being in which we are aware of being) in which change is more possible."

Only in this case it's not your own being, but one of those beings you've created that directly seizes your attention. You're flipping through a magazine, for instance — then a finger seems to abruptly plunge downward, arresting your progress, singling out an image or a few words. That finger belongs to one of your characters; it draws you back into your story and points again toward what you hadn't noticed before. "See the connection," it seems to say. It's Aristotle's "eye for resemblances" once more.

Back at your desk, you may seek quiet and peace in order to write, but don't confuse that with writing in a vacuum. Remember: you never truly write alone. Only now you need to look beyond the fellowship of other writers, the echo of all those clacking keys and scribbling pens. Thomas Wolfe concluded in his preface to *Look Homeward, Angel* that "we are the sum of all the moments of our lives." Your writing too will be the sum of those moments you spent writing and all the moments that came before and led up to the present. Each story is ultimately a filter of all those moments. Of course, you'll also absorb influences from your environment that don't serve your story.

Remember: you never truly write alone.

It's okay: development means eliminating them while remaining open. It's worth the risk. If you permit it to do so, the world will become your teacher. It will teach you about the story you're writing and also about the principal role that storytelling plays in the way we all apprehend reality.

In the seventeenth century, the English philosopher John Locke upheld the argument that the images in our minds duplicate reality as conveyed by the senses, just like the view through a picture window. A century later, however, Immanuel Kant argued that, as scientist Eric R. Kandel says in *The Age of Insight*, "sensory information allows reality to be invented by the mind." And in the twentieth century, Kandel explains, art historians Ernst Kris and Ernst Gombrich applied Kant's ideas to perceptions of art:

> The images in art, like all images, represent not so much reality as the viewer's perceptions, imagination, expectations, and knowledge of other images — images recalled from memory. As Gombrich pointed out, to see what is actually painted on a canvas, the viewer has to know beforehand what he or she might see in a painting.

Gombrich dubbed the role played by inference and invention the "beholder's share": what we bring to art determines what we take from it and how we perceive it in the first place.

In other words, we're constantly looking at the world through portholes formed by our own experience and perceptual habits. What we call perceiving the world actually amounts to our making guesses about it and telling ourselves stories, the accuracy of which we then assess by comparing them with others' stories.

Storytelling, then, is no rarefied art; it's a life skill we all employ to different degrees, purposes, and effects.

Storytelling, then, is no rarefied art; it's a life skill we all employ to different degrees, purposes, and effects. Embrace this knowledge and it will change the way you relate to stories. You'll look up in the middle of conversations or routine behaviors — newly aware that you're participating in a story *and* you're also telling it. Again we've circled back: What does it mean now to recognize yourself as the "decider"?

This back-and-forth between story and life, between perception and reality, can also help you understand just what it means to say that you benefit as a writer each time you cycle through the five stages. The experience you acquire, you reinvest in your work, both consciously and automatically. You discover what works, and then you make it part of yourself. On paper, your characters advance in pursuit of their objectives — but only as you advance in pursuit of yours.

Observing the world through the lens of your stories confers an additional benefit: as you become more attuned to the worlds within worlds, you come to see that there are hundreds, perhaps thousands, of different ways to perceive the same view, the same person, the same experience. Like a disco ball, the world now throws off that much more light as it spins. You know that you can never see it all, but it's enough that you can see.

Oh, the difference between
nearly right and exactly right!

— HORACE J. BROWN

INTRODUCTION

YOU'RE READY FOR THE REFINE STAGE when both your own instincts and the feedback of early readers confirm that your manuscript has fulfilled those goals set forth by your story, in terms of structure, character, plot, theme, and story world. On looking back, you understand that there is no bad writing, only bad timing. You won't declare yourself finished or submit your work until, through acts of creative destruction, you've cut away anything that doesn't serve the story. When overarching story elements no longer need as much attention, you tackle this stage's primary objective: choose the right words.

To do so, you'll need the help of readers and editors whose most constructive feedback can refocus your vision. In this section, we provide more questions for early readers, to complement those we suggested at the Develop stage, as well as guidance on working with an editor. But we also urge you to trust your gut when you weigh the value of conflicting assessments. Finally, we share our thoughts on how time and experience have refined our approaches to the writing itself.

NO BAD WRITING,
ONLY BAD TIMING

Timing has a lot to do with
the outcome of a rain dance.

— ANONYMOUS

As A RULE, your manuscript is ripe for refinement at the point
when your narrative sustains the promise of a dramatically compelling What If question. More specifically, your fully developed
manuscript should exhibit structurally sound storytelling; mul-
tidimensional characters bent on overcoming challenging obstacles in pursuit of meaningful objectives; a credible story world;
and — the dominant element when it comes to expository writing — the logical, engaging progression of strong ideas.

At the Refine stage, you'll focus on language, revising to
amplify your theme or message with more expressive phrasing and eliminate, at the sentence level, all that's unnecessary,
inconsistent, or awkward. In preparation for the Refine stage,
however, we recommend that you step away from your manuscript again. You need that time — and often the feedback of
others — to develop perspective so you can read with fresh eyes.

When you return, you'll have to address all the small
instances of faulty decision making that emerge Loch Ness

Monster–style from your manuscript's surface, undertaking what's referred to in the publishing industry as copyediting. Take heart: the same awareness that illuminates flaws also makes it possible for you to remedy them. A Spanish proverb reminds us that "even the best writer must erase." We can and do erase because we write in sand, not in stone — at least until we submit our final drafts. In the end, it's a matter of timing, of doing it right or doing it over until it's right.

Take heart: the same awareness that illuminates flaws also makes it possible for you to remedy them.

We won't lie to you: doing it over may mean realizing you're not yet done with development. The initial copyedit on *this* book turned out to be an unexpected second round of developmental editing, one for which we felt grateful, once we'd completed those edits. Our own experience points to an uncomfortable truth: far more often than we would like, the fourth stage, Refine (as well as the fifth, Share), doubles as a revolving door. We think we're ready, we hope we're ready — and we plunge into this new cycle of revision, not knowing whether we'll continue onward or find ourselves exiting where we came in, now facing squarely in the opposite direction. Before we attend to the deciding factors, let's take a moment to consider just what might go wrong for any one of us, if only so each of us can feel a little better, a little more optimistic, when we confront the worst-case scenario.

With the noteworthy exception of the insurance-scheme musical *Springtime for Hitler* presented in that classic farce *The Producers*, no one intends for their creation to turn out poorly — so when it does, what might have gone wrong? Generally speaking, we can attribute artistic failure to a lack of experience, patience, or insight, or all three, expressed as some variation on the following: hasty dreaming, hurried drafting, inadequate development, and shallow or ill-considered feedback.

And when the shortcomings become impossible to ignore? There may be times when you recognize your shorter work — and, less frequently though much more painfully, your long-form manuscript — as ill conceived to such a degree that you must abandon it altogether, as many respected authors have done. Producer and musician Sylvia Robinson once observed, "Sometimes strength is holding on, and sometimes letting go." You need not lose hope — letting go may show the way to a more promising project cocooned within the current one. And all the work you put into this project? It will be reflected, subtly if not dramatically, in the next.

Don't be too quick to abandon what you might salvage, no matter how unpleasant the task. But beware of the dismally common conviction that you can conceal flaws at the depths of a manuscript or another project merely by smoothing its surface — in the case of one *Calvin and Hobbes* comic strip, for instance, by enclosing the roughly drafted pages of Calvin's report in a clear plastic binder to deflect the judgment of his teacher. (It's a trick publishers occasionally attempt with a glossy book cover.) Hobbes speaks wisdom for all writers when he responds, "I don't want co-author credit on this, okay?"

Neither do you.

The awful truth bears contemplation: when we refine our work prematurely, our efforts resemble someone trying to turn a plastic spoon into fine silverware by way of a vigorous polishing. On watching a lackluster film or turning the last page of an unsatisfying novel, surely we know better than to blame the costumes or the type design. That's not to say that fashion and fonts don't matter, but we know that their equivalent when it comes to novels or essays cannot compensate for poor development. We must acknowledge at the outset what we can and can't accomplish when we refine: we might be able to handle Nessie, but we can't just ignore the submarine-crunching leviathan that may rise up from a manuscript's depths. In that case, we are going to need a bigger boat. That's right: only rigorous development will naturally lead to refinement.

We must acknowledge at the outset what we can and can't accomplish when we refine.

But what will finally determine whether you'll advance or retreat on leaving that revolving door? Only the feedback you receive from others and your own self-aware, critical judgment. If you haven't done so already, it's now time to seek candid impressions from readers and editors, which will either corroborate or amend your instincts.

The same principles apply not only to creative projects but to communication at large — and the five stages can benefit text messages and tweets as much as essays, short stories, and books, if only because the work you do on one project builds skills that you apply to others. As advertising mogul David Ogilvy emphasized, everyday correspondence also requires patience, self-assessment, and feedback: "Never send an important letter or memo on the day you write it. Read it aloud the next morning, and then edit it. Then ask a colleague to improve it. And do not send it until you make sure it's crystal clear."

The mailbox once brimmed with letters that senders wished they could take back; the Internet makes it even easier to dispatch a message and trigger regret as predictably as a Pavlovian dog's salivation. It's not all bad: In daily life, when we behave badly, we have to make amends. But when we write badly, we need only make edits.

CREATIVE DESTRUCTION

Stick to the point
and whenever you can, cut.

— W. Somerset Maugham

When asked about his technique, a sculptor famous for lifelike depictions of canines said, "I just cut away everything that isn't the dog." We draft and develop in order to clearly identify the dog. When we refine, we cut away everything else. Ideally, you're already telling a good story, but now you strive to do so as efficiently and elegantly as possible. If a sentence expresses an essential idea, advances plot, reveals character, or conveys relevant sensory detail that contributes to emotional effect or atmosphere, then it's probably worth keeping, especially if it achieves more than one of these aims. If not — snip, snip.

Those of us who work with an editor can free our hands (at least temporarily) to cover our eyes as our dispassionate partner hacks away. Sometimes an editor's judicious slashing of words alone can liberate a readable and powerful narrative from a meandering, disorganized draft. The skilled copyeditor strives for economy of expression on the writer's behalf — something you'll want to remember on return of your manuscript, which may at first seem truncated or otherwise mutilated. William Strunk and E. B. White's *The Elements of Style* advises, "Omit needless words....A sentence should contain no unnecessary words, a paragraph no unnecessary sentences, for the same reason that a drawing should have no unnecessary lines and a machine no unnecessary parts." The golden thread of each story also embodies this law of necessity.

Whether or not you work with an editor, you'll always have to serve as your own editor. You cultivate a healthy detachment when you acknowledge that your first choice of words is expendable in the service of your story. Refinement requires ongoing vigilance: take a step back periodically and consider the manuscript as a whole, at the section or chapter level, as well as at the paragraph and sentence level. Look for false beginnings or endings — the opening and close of the manuscript need to coincide with the beginning and end of the story and not prolong the narrative beyond these two points. And be aware that one or more of your subplots, no matter how beautifully composed, may not serve your story: *Is it inevitable or arbitrary?* Does it meaningfully connect with the story's golden thread? Does it contribute to some larger understanding that the reader would otherwise have trouble grasping?

Your first choice of words is expendable in the service of your story.

Next, zoom in once more. Tongue firmly in cheek, English writer Sydney Smith advised, "In composing, run your pen through every other word you have written; you have no idea what vigor it will give your style." Follow the spirit of Smith's advice and you'll surely eliminate some adjectives and adverbs (such as *vehemently* in "he blurted vehemently"), which often fail to meet the test of necessity because they slow down the reader. In other words, whenever you can say what you need to say in fewer words, do it, because simplicity is power.

Whenever you can say what you need to say in fewer words, do it, because simplicity is power.

Your capacity for creative destruction will develop like any other — with time and experience. For immediate guidance on how to proceed, subject your draft's every paragraph, sentence, and word to a three-question test: *Can it be written more aptly? Can it be written more briefly? Does it need to be written at all?*

You can ease your way by cutting any sentence or paragraph that you're not sure works and pasting or copying it elsewhere. Once that newly orphaned extract has found a safe refuge, a halfway house to your archives, you can return to your draft and see how it reads. Rest assured that you can always add back the deleted material in some other form, in the same or a more appropriate location. It's not that difficult to let go of what doesn't work, but it's tougher to relinquish what works in favor of what works better, and to sacrifice even that for what works best. That's the kind of cutting that confers refinement on a draft.

Elmore Leonard once suggested that all you have to do is "cut out the parts people skip over." Authors actually cut for three overlapping reasons: to serve the story, to serve the market, and to serve the reader. Journalist Gaiutra Bahadur, while editing *Coolie Woman*, expressed in a Facebook post her heartfelt frustration at necessary cuts:

Trying not to cry too much over the 2,500 word section of the book I just had to let go: an evocation of the world of Henry Bullock, Berbice overseer from 1860 to 1890. Trying also not to cry over the 300 letters of his — in crab-like, sideways, sometimes illegible scrawl — that I digitized and read and indexed and cross-referenced over many hundreds of hours to evoke his world, which nobody's ever evoked before.

As Bahadur's post illustrates, refining with publication in mind can mean making cuts that bolster your manuscript without necessarily serving the overall story in which you're immersed. You'll hear this again: it's your manuscript but the publisher's book. At the behest of Scribner editor Maxwell Perkins, Thomas Wolfe agreed to cut more than sixty thousand words from the novel ultimately published in 1929 as *Look Homeward, Angel*. Wolfe later broke with Perkins over those cuts. In 2000, the University of South Carolina Press published a more lightly edited version of his original manuscript as *O Lost: A Story of the Buried Life*, Wolfe's original title; it remains in print though also obscure to all but Wolfe's most loyal admirers. (For better or worse, the author's cut has not yet become a niche genre in the way the director's cut has in film.)

When Robert Caro submitted the manuscript of *The Power Broker* to Bob Gottlieb, his editor at Knopf, he learned that he would have to cut three hundred thousand words. "That's like cutting a five-hundred-page book out of a book," he told the *Paris Review*. After that initial cut, Gottlieb then told him they'd have to cut fifty thousand more words. "I could have read twice as much," Gottlieb said later, "but I couldn't print twice as much." Gottlieb might have been willing to read more, but he presumably didn't think enough people would be willing to pay an obligatory forty-five dollars to do so.

Cutting doesn't necessarily signal failure or surrender on the writer's part. Elie Wiesel points to the "difference between a book of two hundred pages from the very beginning, and a book of two hundred pages which is the result of an original eight hundred pages." As Wiesel explains, "The six hundred pages are there, you only don't see them." Sometimes text cut from one book may give rise to another book, even more than one. Alternatively, you may cut material in one form but alter other text subtly so that it suggests what's been cut — thrifty and crafty.

You don't have to go online or to a bookstore, however, to realize that overcutting is rare while overwriting is epidemic. So heed the rule "When in doubt, cut it out." Amen to that.

OBJECTIVE:
CHOOSE THE RIGHT WORDS

An honest tale speeds best,
being plainly told.

— WILLIAM SHAKESPEARE

WHEN WE TALK ABOUT "the right words at the right time," we're alluding to the story evoked by these words, the context for events, encounters, and ideas. It's the story that makes the words right, and you make your own story right by developing it as fully as possible. After you've conceived and ordered the vital ideas that form that story's golden thread, it's time for you to devote yourself wholeheartedly to crafting language that fully embodies those ideas, the objective of the Refine stage. That last enveloping layer, the right words, will make your story seamless.

Now you consider whether the words to which you've so far entrusted your story are the best ones to convey it. In response, you cut words, alter or reorder them, and add more as necessary. Or you leave them alone. At this point, we need to throw back the curtain of mystic awe that generally obscures working with words; it's a sentiment evoked, though not necessarily endorsed, by readers who say they read "for language." To understand why such readers are only telling half the story, and the less revealing half at that, we need to establish a few points.

First, let's acknowledge that language has a particular function: in the broadest sense, we use it to convey what we intend to be comprehensible messages, whether fact or fiction. Grammar and punctuation are tools that serve this purpose, comparable with the tongue of a diplomat who reconciles warring tribes on the eve of battle or the legs of the Greek messenger whose legendary run gave rise to the marathon.

In school, you may have copied out definitions and diagrammed sentences in order to "build your vocabulary" and "learn good grammar." Did you understand then that these are means and not ends in themselves? We each need a rich vocabulary, in order to express a full range of thoughts and feelings, and a strong grasp of grammar and punctuation, in order to do so with clarity and elegance. If you were lucky, you had a teacher who made it clear that punctuation influences meaning. Perhaps he wrote on the board these two famed variations on the same phrase:

Woman, without her man, is lost.
Woman! Without her — man is lost.

Whether in or beyond the classroom, none of us write to "communicate clearly"; we write first to figure out what we need to say and then to do so with all the power and grace we can muster.

When you tell stories and explore ideas, a functional command of grammar and punctuation (far more than any knowledge of linguistic terminology)

> **We write first to figure out what we need to say and then to do so with all the power and grace we can muster.**

will enable you to put language at the service of a handful of discrete objectives: to advance plot, reveal character, arouse emotion and sensation, and convey information the reader needs in order to appreciate the story. All of these are equally important, but without one of them, language cannot truly sing. Poet and memoirist Mary Karr makes it clear just which one is "primary" in the essay "Against Decoration," included with her collection of poems *Viper Rum*:

> I always thought that poetry's primary purpose was to stir emotion, and that one's delight in dense idiom or syntax or allusion served a secondary one. I don't mind, for instance, working hard to read *Paradise Lost*, because I return to Milton for the terror and hubris Satan embodies....One can with perfect legitimacy use a reference or create an elaborately metaphoric or linguistic surface in a poem. But when those elements become final ends, rather than acting as a conduit for a range of feelings, poetry ceases to perform its primary function: to move the reader.

Perhaps the writer who reads "for language" recognizes that some words make us feel more than others because they are the right words at the right time and because they strike us as inevitable — in our hearts and in our bones. As Mark Twain put it, "The difference between the almost right word and the right word is really a large matter — it's the difference between the lightning bug and the lightning."

Some words strike us as inevitable — in our hearts and in our bones.

As you now know, the writer doubles as a conductor of emotion. When we refine, we turn our attention to pace, rhythm, and cadence. Through your own reading, you've likely already discovered that long sentences and dense vocabulary generally slow pace, whereas shorter sentences and simpler words accelerate it. Two sentences may express an idea equally well, but imagine that only one of them manages to balance acceleration and delay so as to produce the suspenseful effect you desire — pace then becomes the deciding factor. That's the kind of choice you make, whether consciously or automatically, when you refine.

In music, cadence refers to a repeated melody or rhythm that signals an ending. When we hear a guitarist play a song in the key of C, for instance, we seem to need that C chord evoked once more at the song's end; with it comes a settling of the soul.

The discerning reader becomes aware of a comparable effect at moments of transition within a story or at the story's end. According to one tale, possibly apocryphal, the twin brothers who first scripted *Casablanca* had trouble resolving a penultimate scene; inspiration struck them simultaneously while they were driving, and they turned to each other and said at once, "Round up the usual suspects!" They knew that the repetition of that line in a new, more developed context would create the sense of the story having come full circle. We can credit cadence for the power of this and many other famous scenes in the history of cinema and literature.

When you refine, you aim to draw what you've learned into alignment with your instincts, to summon the right words to mind and to recognize them as such. That undertaking will remain mysterious to some extent — though you may find a thesaurus helpful — but you can ease your way, yet again, by asking questions. This time, as you closely review your manuscript, assess the purpose of each sentence, each paragraph, asking yourself:

❖ Does the text advance plot?
❖ Does it reveal character?
❖ Does it arouse emotion and sensation?
❖ Does it convey necessary information?

Some sentences may achieve one or more of the preceding aims but in a way better accomplished by other, more necessary sentences. In that case, you know the rule: snip, snip.

Refining often finishes with the last and first lines, the links that resolve the story's circle at the mouth of the labyrinth. In every great story, the beginning must contain the end, and the end in turn points toward the beginning — a circularity and sense of completion that we can experience in literature even if not in life.

Ford Madox Ford's novel *The Good Soldier* opens with an unforgettable first line: "This is the saddest story I have ever heard." From just nine words, we learn that the novel has a sensitive, first-person narrator who will tell us a story that's likely to move us because it has moved him more than any other. When you refine, your story becomes a boat that you row closer and closer to the shore where your readers wait. You want to move so close that they can reach out and grasp your outstretched hands, and if you do the work, they won't ever want to let go.

QUESTIONS: MORE TO ASK
EARLY READERS

I learned to ask readers, "Tell me how you reacted,
not what you think ought to be done."
Because very often people will jump to
their sense of what needs to be fixed
and bypass the initial reader's perception
of what was lacking in his experience.
Also, I'm usually better at fixing
my own writing than they are.

— MICHAEL CRICHTON

IT'S COMMON FOR WRITERS to slap a manuscript into a willing friend's or colleague's hands as though it were a subpoena, then run like hell before he changes his mind. Okay, maybe not exactly, but bear with us. After the handoff, a couple of weeks of hand-wringing likely follow. Then comes the predictable phone call and a few minutes of nervous small talk leading up to the inevitable question: "What did you think?" Even a beat or two of awkward silence may strain the relationship, and it probably won't help the manuscript.

For that reason, we propose a different choice: a printed questionnaire for readers, intended to accompany your manuscript like a cover letter. You can best demonstrate your gratitude toward willing readers by — as made plain in an earlier chapter — helping them help you. We recommend you look upon the following list as a first layer of your own lineup of manuscript-specific questions intended to focus your early readers' attention and help them translate their potentially nebulous impressions into fruitful commentary. Many readers not comfortable with line editing can still offer valuable big-picture impressions. Those of us who understand that it's part of our work to keep you writing are the ones to whom you'll want to return. Ideally, the questionnaire will serve as the basis for a longer, in-person conversation.

Instruct your readers to peruse these questions *before* they start reading your manuscript and to return to them afterward.

1. After you've read the full manuscript, please step away for a few days. Now, presuming you've done so: *What do you then recall of the story's events? Please summarize in writing all that you can recall of the major events of the story — including its beginning and ending — without consulting the manuscript.* This summary may be one of the most valuable tasks your readers can perform for you, because it will tell you if the reader is reading the same story you think you're writing. When you refine, you may still need to determine whether your text begins at the appropriate moment — as soon as possible before the major events of the story commence. The reader's summary may indicate excess introductory text or that a subplot repeatedly overlooked may not belong in the story. That said, less perceptive readers may only repeat back to you what you've written, regardless of whether

your story truly begins with the first line of your current text.

2. *On returning to the manuscript, imagine that you'd come across it, not knowing who wrote it. Out of idle curiosity, you flipped it open and read the first line — would it make you want to read on if you had no other reason to do so? Does reading the first paragraph make you more likely to want to continue? Why or why not?* Up until you begin to refine, the first line of text is a placeholder. At this point, however, you'll want to give it more attention, along with your first paragraph, which can stand in for the overall story. In an interview with the *Paris Review*, the novelist Gabriel García Márquez said, "In the first paragraph you solve most of the problems with your book. The theme is defined, the style, the tone. At least in my case, the first paragraph is a kind of sample of what the rest of the book is going to be." Also, remember to periodically remind your readers that you want their subjective impressions and opinions. And don't forget to ask why, even if it seems implicit.

3. *At which points in the text, if any, did you have to stop and go back to reread?* Clarity matters. Make it clear to your readers that their honesty as to their own lack of understanding will help you and that you will not judge them for it.

4. *What did the story make you feel and at what point? With which characters did you sympathize? Whom did you want*

to succeed? Whom did you dislike? Why? As long as you're working on a manuscript, you never stop trying to move the reader. It's up to you to determine whether answers to this question point to a need for a change in wording or plotting — remember that the Refine stage can act as a revolving door, meaning that your manuscript may still need development. In some instances, like this one, multiple readers' reactions will likely serve you more than one individual's answers.

5.   *At what points, if any, did you have trouble believing what happened? What do you think made you doubt?* This question applies to both nonfiction and fiction — not everything true is automatically believable. On a different note, the phrasing of this question purposely anticipates negative feedback so as to reassure readers nervous about delivering it. "It's okay," you should tell your readers. "I want your candor, and I appreciate it." Readers may have trouble explaining the basis for a particular impression, but it's still worth asking them to try doing so, in part because it may help you narrow down whether the problem lies with the plot point itself, its translation into text, or the characters participating in it. Make it clear when you give your early readers the questionnaire, however, just how valuable their impressions alone will be to you.

6.   *Did the story world (or setting) feel like a real place to you? If yes, do you recall any particular description or details that made it so? If not, where in the text did you find a clear*

sense of place lacking? If you're setting your story in a real place, we advise you to find one or more readers who know that place well, so their critiques can double as a kind of research on your part. On the other hand, readers who haven't visited the place may be less likely to compare it with, say, *their* Montreal or to get lost in issues of minute accuracy that may or may not matter to your story. Additionally, text on the page is anything but a purely visual experience. Your language should convey a full-bodied sensory experience — though erotica and biography may require different varieties of experience — and your readers can help you ensure that it does.

7. *Did any specific words or phrases detract from the story, either because you couldn't understand them or because they pulled you out of the text and slowed you down? Please mark any such sections in the manuscript.* You may want to explicitly ask your readers to review at least a portion of the text two or more times — the shorter the whole piece, the more likely they are to agree. An image that impresses readers as "wonderful" during the first read may strike them as "not quite appropriate" on the second pass when it sinks back into the text (and context) from which it had previously leaped. Even those of your readers who don't consider themselves editors probably won't find it too difficult to highlight a problematic phrase or sentence in the text and then explain themselves more generally in the body of the questionnaire.

Finally, make it explicit that you welcome general impressions from your readers. The questions are there to encourage and guide feedback, not to restrict it. Even readers unwilling or unable to answer all of the above questions may be able to offer valuable feedback. And they may also help you revise your questionnaire. Doing so as frequently as necessary becomes part of your process.

WORKING WITH AN EDITOR

Bob [Gottlieb] will say to me...these pages, for me,
they're too lyrical, too self-conscious....
I disagree because I'm in love with every word I've written,
but I'll rake it over and lick my wounds....
In no case have I ever regretted taking Bob's advice.

— JOHN LE CARRÉ

IN THE COURSE OF YOUR WRITING VENTURES, you'll likely encounter two different types of editors and enjoy a different relationship with each. When you sign a contract, your publisher will assign you an in-house editor, but most writers, and all self-published authors, work exclusively with freelancers, independent contractors hired by you to help you develop your work. Unless funds are no obstacle, we recommend you first seek feedback from friends and acquaintances. And you'll want to think carefully about when to seek editorial guidance and what kind you need.

Freelance editors provide a variety of services, ranging from big-picture developmental review to line-by-line editing and proofreading. Many authors double as freelancers, and some market themselves as ghostwriters or cowriters. For the most part, it's an uncomplicated relationship: we employ freelancers, and they do the best they can for us, depending on our mutual experience and skill. A basic online search will put you in touch with a legion of independent editors, but we recommend you seek out a personal referral from a fellow writer or a local publisher or literary agency. Your editor doesn't need to be local; in fact, someone you never meet face to face may better stand in for all those faceless readers.

If you seek a developmental overview, the freelancer will prepare a report of five pages or more that assesses the strengths and weaknesses of your story structure, character development, theme, story world, and use of language, making suggestions for improvement whenever possible. Take care not to confuse applied knowledge of writing principles with expertise on the publishing industry. Even those freelance editors who've worked in the industry generally don't make predictions as to whether rights to your work will be acquired by a traditional publisher, but they can help you increase the likelihood of reaching, and pleasing, your intended audience.

Freelance editors generally don't make predictions, but they can help you increase the likelihood of reaching, and pleasing, your intended audience.

Line editing and copyediting aren't strictly identical but, for practical purposes, they blend into each other — and individual editors' approaches vary widely. Some editors may do little rewriting and more proofreading, following specific rules of grammar and style. Others will intervene more, doing minor reworking and cutting, as well as helping to clarify confusing, dense, or rambling text, eliminating awkwardness in diction or sentence structure, and correcting grammar and punctuation in order to further refine your work.

The same editor may undertake a developmental review, surveying your work through a telescope, and later line edit or copyedit your manuscript, swapping a telescope for a magnifying glass. The professional hired to line edit or copyedit will want to begin by marking up a sample of ten or so pages, most likely electronically, unless you and the editor agree to mark edits on a paper copy of the manuscript. That initial sample edit informs editors as to the density and style of your work and enables them to project their expenditure of time and your total cost for the project. It will also give you a sense of their skills and help you decide if you'd like to work with them. As in any working relationship, you'll want to assess their clarity of communication, honesty, timeliness, and personality — whether you are likely to get along well. It's always a good idea to ask for references from their recent clients.

Whether you want a developmental review or a copyedit, don't hesitate to engage multiple editors in discussion before you choose one. In the former case, you should request a sample of their developmental work. Ask them about their specializations, keeping in mind that few people do everything well. As Will Rogers said, "Everyone is ignorant, only on different subjects." All editors should be able to identify challenges, but some may be more adept at proposing solutions or rewriting.

We highly recommend that you work together to draw up and sign a letter of agreement stating your mutual expectations and goals. It's not intended as a legal document but rather to translate assumptions into written understandings that inspire trust based upon clear communication. (For the same reason, such a written agreement is even more essential when you are collaborating with a coauthor.)

If a traditional publishing house acquires your manuscript, you will form a professional relationship with an in-house editor, usually the editor who acquired and championed the book, but not always. For the most part, you won't choose an editor; rather, that editor will choose you — or, more specifically, your proposal or manuscript. On some occasions, an editor acquires rights to a book only to move on to another house or career, in which case you and your book are handed off to another editor on staff. It's worth noting that in-house editors don't work for you. Neither do you work for them, though it may feel like you do when they assign you fact-checking tasks and request that you respond to queries and edits before they accept the final manuscript.

It's important to discuss your work with your editor and to tactfully express any concerns about your working relationship as they arise. Preoccupied with business concerns and editorial duties related to other books on their seasonal list, in-house editors may seem elusive at times, and the relationship can become more complicated, shifting from amicable to adversarial, especially with a first-time author who may understandably expect more special attention — such as extended telephone calls — than the editor can give. Bear in mind that your editor is neither a psychological counselor nor a personal friend, although some may seem to occasionally take on these roles.

An agent may be able to help resolve misunderstandings or disagreements about cover art or marketing. In-house editors usually welcome your input, but they have the final say about the title, cover, and design elements. Once again: you created and own the manuscript; the publisher produces and owns the rights to the physical (and in most cases the digital) book.

You created and own the manuscript; the publisher produces and owns the rights to the physical (and in most cases the digital) book.

Most likely, your editor's suggestions will help you develop a better book, but that doesn't mean you need to rubber-stamp every suggested change. Remember: edits made by an in-house editor are suggestions, not commands. However, if you reject major editorial suggestions, that editor has the option to decline to publish your book. As your intermediary with the publisher, your editor is the servant of two masters and has reason to echo that impassioned plea we heard first from fictional sports agent Jerry Maguire, speaking to football player Rod Tidwell: "Help *me* help *you*!"

Ideally, you won't content yourself with making only those changes your editor suggests but will treat the editorial overview as a jumping-off point for another, more self-directed layer of revision. Your editor may identify a problem only once that actually repeats itself throughout the book. Or the request that you add a sentence of explanation may point to the need to rewrite the entire paragraph in which it's embedded. If additional changes make the manuscript better — with one important caveat that we get to in the last chapter of this stage — then your editor will appreciate the added effort.

Your relationship with your editor, whether freelance or in-house, is ultimately like any other relationship — it's what you make of it. The publishing industry has changed dramatically in the past few decades and will continue to reinvent itself. Despite ongoing concern over dwindling profits and attention spans, the mission remains the same for you both: to produce the kind of books that made you want to write your own.

TRUST YOUR GUT

First you jump off the cliff,
and you grow your wings on the way down.

— RAY BRADBURY

WHEN YOU DREAM AND DRAFT, your trust resembles faith, but when you develop and refine, trust acts in concert with your critical judgment. It's not because you've ceased to trust yourself that you ask others to read and respond to your work. On the contrary, your wrestling with others' feedback will at once refine your instincts and your ability to evaluate critiques and suggestions and to resolve contradictions.

What if, for instance, your agent raves about the same chapter in your book that your editor urges you to cut? Or if two equally credible readers express polar-opposite opinions about a plot point or character choice? Whom can you trust in these instances? When it comes time to make a decision, you *must* trust your gut because no one knows your story better than you do — and because you get to know your work in a new way as you thoughtfully integrate the feedback you receive.

"If you can tell the difference between good advice and bad advice," the adage goes, "then you don't need advice." The preceding statement holds some wisdom, though you may have to pry open its fingers to get at it: you come to distinguish good from bad advice by taking advice and learning from the consequences how to better listen to your own intuition.

As Billy Wilder said, "Trust your own instincts. Your mistakes might as well be your own instead of someone else's." Constructive feedback echoes your own innate sense of *what* you want to convey and *how* you wish to express it, though that feedback may so thoroughly transform one or the other as to leave you slack jawed, starry-eyed, and, eventually, grateful.

> Constructive feedback echoes your own innate sense of *what* you want to convey and *how* you wish to express it,

Some feedback will immediately strike you as apt, perhaps because you've anticipated it but wanted confirmation. It may be expressed in such a way that it allows you to see your current draft through new eyes. Or it may occasionally feel like a punch to the gut that you want to ignore but can't. And you shouldn't because this last kind of feedback may have the most value, even if — especially if — it sends you back to development, where you can then make better use of your time.

Conversely, some feedback will quickly expose itself as inappropriate, even absurd. In a work of memoir anthologized in *The May Queen*, the Moroccan American novelist and essayist Laila Lalami describes a creative writing workshop in which she remained silent while others critiqued her work (as is customary). A couple of her classmates had trouble focusing on her story:

> "I liked your story," he said, "but, well, I thought it didn't have enough detail. For example, you mention in passing a rug under the table. But Morocco has such

beautiful rugs. And you don't describe this one!" A woman sitting at the other end of the table nodded her head vigorously. "You have to make the most of your exotic setting."

At first, Lalami tried to incorporate more "exotic" detail into her story, but gradually she realized that doing so would mean further propping up stereotypes and that it would prevent her from ever producing books that honored the truth of her own experience.

When you're called to evaluate ambiguous feedback, first consider the person giving it. We've advised you about when, what, and whom to ask, but you can learn yet more about the critic from the critique — the more you know about the messenger, the better you can appraise the value of the message.

The more you know about the messenger, the better you can appraise the value of the message.

One question matters more than any other: *Does this reader belong to my target audience?* If a reader suggests major changes, for instance, or finds your work "inappropriate," it may be relevant that she tore herself away from yet another volume of literary criticism in order to peruse your romance-suspense mash-up. And then the question becomes, Why did you approach this reader in the first place? Perhaps she's a fellow writer who has given you valuable feedback in the past. Take that into account too.

In an ideal world, your first readers would fall into a circle delineated by your ideal readers. Take note: if you're writing a young-adult novel, you'll want to find some young adults to read your manuscript. In the preface to her memoir *Committed*, Elizabeth Gilbert names twenty-seven readers for whom she wrote the book. When any one of those women gave her sincere feedback, she had good reason to listen.

At the same time, readers who know you well — even classmates, after a short time — may start to bring what they know about you and what they want from you to the text itself, potentially distorting their feedback. For instance, classmates sitting across the table from you in a memoir writing class probably won't notice that you don't actually establish the gender of your first-person narrator until your second page.

Friends and classmates eager to get to know you might read your essay in full when, if they'd merely come across it online, they'd skim or even abandon it after a sentence or two. Stay alert to the possibility of this type of distortion; listen carefully to what your readers say — and what they don't say — and evaluate all feedback critically, whether it's negative or positive. It's important because when we write for the wider community of readers, we also write for strangers.

To expand upon a previous point, sometimes we need feedback solely to provoke a reaction that points us in the right direction. For instance, you don't need to believe in a Magic 8 Ball to make use of it. Ask a question and gauge your emotional response to the outcome: Are you relieved or crestfallen? Perhaps you decide to try again. And again. Until you receive the desired answer. (If you don't have an 8 Ball handy, you can always flip a coin and notice how your reaction to the heads or tails reveals what you wanted or hoped for from the start.)

Finally, you need to rely on your self-knowledge to divine the significance of your emotional responses. The imperative to trust your gut builds upon layers of intuition and analysis, as well as a willingness to draw upon them. And only by using your gut can you confirm that it's worth trusting.

SIERRA: HOW I WRITE NOW

In a Norwegian fairy tale, the hero came to
a crossroads where there are three signs:
"He who travels down this road will return unharmed";
"He who travels this path may or may not return"; and,
"He who travels here will never return."
Of course, he chose the third.

— LAURA SIMMS

WHEN I PRACTICE YOGA, I strive to breathe deeply and peacefully while contorting myself into a series of stress positions. When I write now, I seem to do the opposite. I situate myself as comfortably as possible so as to support the inner struggle because writing necessitates a war within, but I am not the enemy. Only after years of experimentation do I understand this fully, and I choose what works for me in the moment. I refine my process as necessary, and it continually refines me.

The French writer and actor Sacha Guitry wrote that "our wisdom comes from our experience, and our experience comes from our foolishness." Younger and more foolish, I once walked the path of the self-flagellant, guided by the notion that discipline meant forcing myself to write under even the most strenuous circumstances, grimacing through the practice, and pretending myself content with feelings of relief when I finally turned in a writing assignment.

In those days, I either resisted any change to how I wrote, resenting any contrary signals from my environment, or tried to emulate practices that I blindly accepted as superior without contemplating the precise reasoning behind them: writing in cafés, for instance, or by hand, entirely because writers I admired did so. When I sat down in those cafés, I noticed that they were noisy and distracting. When I tried handwriting instead of typing, I couldn't seem to relax my hand, and it soon began to ache. I wrote less and read more, because reading gave me the feeling of writing and required only that I shrug off the attendant guilt. *Someday*, I thought, then I turned the page.

Now I read somewhat less and write more. I generally prefer a laptop and mostly reject a traditional desk for a lap desk that rests on my thighs as I sit cross-legged on my bed. When I can't write at home — it's still my first choice — I'll write in a café, on a plane, even seated on a bench at a museum. I can do so because I've become less vulnerable to distraction over time and because I no longer expect where I write to motivate me to do the writing. I now prefer to compose letters and journal entries by hand. I dreamt up the story to my in-progress novel in a notebook, the old-fashioned kind.

What changed? I did. Life put me in all kinds of stress positions, as it does all of us, and I gradually concluded that if I couldn't free myself from those positions, then I could at least release all unnecessary tension. And when I could free myself, I did so as quickly as possible.

I've become more comfortable with being comfortable, because the release of bad tension diverts energy toward maintaining good tension.

I've become more comfortable with being comfortable, because the release of bad tension diverts energy toward maintaining good tension. Constructive relaxation doesn't put me to sleep — it liberates my mind to seek challenge and adventure when I write.

Even in those years when I didn't write nearly as often as I desired, I couldn't forget that I wanted to write more, and I never stopped trying to make it happen. The revelation came when I realized that discipline is whatever we do to make it easier to return to the practice, whereas we may otherwise look on a disciplined person as a stubborn masochist, enviable, perhaps, but also alien. I discovered that I could make even difficult tasks and pursuits, like running, more appealing, while accomplishing and even exceeding the outcomes I expected. Who knew that just running *more slowly* would enable me to run longer and farther with time?

As an adult, it helped to turn my bed into a desk, in the same way it had helped me to do my homework at the kitchen table as an elementary school student: I'm hardly the first writer to actively define writing as inhabiting a midpoint between work and play. As I write more, the pull of some projects has become so strong that I can sit down with them anywhere, and nothing short of outright disaster can disrupt the trance that enfolds me.

As for writing longhand, I'd kept sporadic journals as a teenager and long desired a regular practice. The advantages of journaling on computer also turned out to be disadvantages: the limitless blank space in which to write threatened to turn the practice into a time-consuming indulgence, and the ease of editing almost immediately became a prompt *to* edit, irreconcilable with pure expression. But it became possible for me to write by hand only when, starting a few years ago, I changed my pen and my grip. The pen I use now requires less pressure, and holding it between index and middle fingers enables me to release the tension that previously fatigued my hand.

I decided to write only half a page a day for a couple of months so as to make journaling as easy as possible. Next I permitted myself to write a full page, suspecting that the daily repetition — in contrast with earlier, more sporadic efforts — would create familiarity, then comfort, then desire, and then need. Nowadays I no longer journal every day. Sometimes I write three days in a row; other times, I let a week go by — and that's okay because it's what I need now.

When I began writing a novel in 2011, I discovered that writing longhand helped me dream with drafting in mind, and I filled three notebooks with free-associative story summaries and character biographies. It made a certain kind of editing almost impossible and enabled me to concentrate entirely on cultivating and defining story. When it came time to draft, I quickly returned to the computer. Before stepping away to work on this book, I wrote 150 pages of that novel draft without ever looking back at all my notes; strangely and perfectly, I hadn't written them to be read.

> Writing longhand made a certain kind of editing almost impossible and enabled me to concentrate entirely on cultivating and defining story.

Eventually, on Paul Theroux's advice and on my own instincts, I may return to longhand. "I often recopy a page by hand, to improve it and get into the mood," Theroux wrote in the *Wall Street Journal* last year. Just as reading an almost finished piece aloud helps me hear any false notes in its music and rhythm, in refining by hand, I believe I'll feel the bumps and ridges that still need to be smoothed away. I understand now just why it's useful to be able to write anywhere — anything that permits more writing time — and by hand, an underappreciated art that resonates in the brain differently than typing. Both have become an integral, personal part of my practice because I've made them so.

Looking back, I have trouble seeing my earlier choices as mistakes because they led me to where I find myself now. In forcing myself to write more, I made writing more comfortable. In that time, as a dedicated fool, I set myself on a path toward wisdom.

DAN: MY FINAL DRAFT

It is perfectly okay to write garbage
as long as you edit brilliantly.

— C. J. CHERRYH

IT TOOK ME SEVEN YEARS to complete my first book, writing in starts and stops for an hour or two each day. My second book, start to finish, took me three months of fourteen-hour days. In each case, the books went through dreaming, drafting, developing, and refining before it was time to share. For these first books, and every one that's always followed, the draft I'm writing has always felt like the most difficult one — but, for me, the final draft poses the greatest emotional challenge.

The *first draft* is a sheer muscular effort, like running an ultramarathon or building a massive stone wall. This analogy falls short because I know that I can complete a race or build a wall by applying will and effort — one step, one stone at a time. But when faced with the specter of an unwritten manuscript, I just never know. Every day, I return to another blank page waiting for me to pick up where I left off and trek on into uncharted territory. A good outline may dull the knife-edge of doubt, but no preparations I undertake can erase the existential fact: I must create something out of nothing.

I know that I can complete a race or build a wall by applying will and effort. But when faced with the specter of an unwritten manuscript, I just never know.

The completed first draft has the heft of a book, but I pass through this oasis as if it were a mirage. After a brief or sometimes extended respite, I tackle the *second* draft, which requires that I confront serious questions: *Is this really the book I want to write? If not, what must be done?* I throw out everything I don't absolutely need and set about organizing the rest. It's easier than it used to be. In precomputer days, I once taped every single page of a manuscript into continuous scrolls that covered nearly every floor surface in our apartment. Then, over two intensive days, I crawled over the pages, cutting away certain sections with scissors; then I moved and pasted them elsewhere with clear tape before reassembling and retyping this patchwork into the next, cleaner draft.

At some point, I may set aside the manuscript yet again because I know that the *third* draft is critical. Here I must confront the need for development. The feedback from my early readers helps me determine whether the manuscript needs a minor or major rewrite. If all goes well, I find myself writing sentences, expressing ideas, developing nuances of narrative that I simply couldn't have realized in earlier layers.

Then comes a *fourth* draft, and sometimes a *fifth* or *sixth*, which is the one I will submit to my agent or publisher. They will either accept it as is or send it back to me with concerns, queries, and editorial suggestions. I hope that my editor will catch what I've missed and protect me from looking like the hack that I secretly fear I may be. I remind myself that few book manuscripts are ever finished — they're only surrendered. In my case, not without a fight. I review every word again, refining each sentence and paragraph, making adjustments and cutting where I can, guided by the words of writer and journalist François Gautier: "More important than the quest for certainty is the quest for clarity."

By this time, I've lived with the ideas and characters so intensely, so intimately, that we need a break from each other. My objectivity is shot; I'm done with the manuscript, but it's not yet done with me. I still need to review the typeset galleys or book proofs, and sign off, finally dispatching the nearly finished book to proofreading and production. Except that the typeset text always reveals flaws that were invisible before: phrases that now seem awkward and need to be rewritten or cut, a missing transitional sentence, and punctuation that's not quite right. That story about Proust agonizing all day over a comma begins to make sense to me. With a certain obsessive-compulsive élan, I dive into last-minute refinements.

That story about Proust agonizing all day over a comma begins to make sense to me.

There's something about seeing my writing in its typeset form that calls forth memories of wonderful works with which my book now suffers in comparison. Or maybe I'm reluctant to let go because I know this is my last chance, my last dance.

I know that some degree of this final-draft syndrome happens to other authors. Publishers know it so well that most include a clause in the contract to the effect that if the author wishes to make more than a few minor corrections, he must pay for the privilege. These final proofs mark the official shift from manuscript to book; the transfer of ownership from writer to publisher; and the transformation of writer into author.

I've frequently made so many changes to galleys that they come to resemble an early draft assaulted by a guerrilla copy-editor. In the aftermath of one such dispatch, I received a fax from my editor with a photo likeness of a young Clint Eastwood as the tough cop Dirty Harry. The image shows him holding up a smoking gun, and my editor had scrawled beneath the photo, "Go ahead — make one more change..." I sensed she was bluffing.

If only the birds sang that sing the sweetest,
the woods would be silent.

— PROVERB

INTRODUCTION

WITH THE SHARE STAGE, your project concludes but your journey continues as you let the world know about your work. Today, you can share that work in unprecedented ways, according to your aspirations, and connect with ever-larger and more diverse audiences.

Even as publishing and distribution technologies evolve, your objective remains the same, building on your labors in the first four stages: it's time to move your readers to buy, read, and recommend your work.

When you can summarize the dramatic core of your story by describing your book in brief, then you'll be ready to approach agents, editors, journalists, and bloggers. All of us, including established professionals, must occasionally deal with rejection, and you can take consolation and encouragement from fellow writers' war stories. At this stage, you'll be faced with a fundamental decision as to whether or not to self-publish your book. Should you opt for a traditional publisher, we offer an insider's view of the nine-sale gauntlet that your book must traverse on the road to publication and beyond. Whatever path you choose, you'll need to know how to market both your book and yourself. Finally, through stories drawn from our own careers, we explore sharing on the web and perspectives on the writing life.

OBJECTIVE: MOVE YOUR READERS

Writing is perhaps the greatest of human inventions,
binding together people who never knew each other,
citizens of distant epochs.
Books break the shackles of time.
A book is proof that humans are capable
of working magic.

— CARL SAGAN

WE ALL DO THE WORK of authors now. Across the planet, on a daily basis, we're moved to compose and share words, images, and sounds with crowds of friends, acquaintances, and strangers, promoting our own and others' work to an ever-expanding web of connections.

As a writer who aspires to share your own work, you'll contend with greater competition for attention than ever before, yet it's also easier to tap into a worldwide hunger for good stories. With the right words at the right time, you can conceivably develop a following in places you might never physically travel.

Whether you entrust your work to a traditional publisher or go your own way — curating, blogging, vlogging, posting to

213

Facebook, tweeting, or contributing to a proliferating legion of online publications — your objective in the Share stage remains the same: to enthrall and inform readers and to move them to send your work rippling outward across and beyond their own networks.

This fifth stage transcends the four preceding ones only to the extent that it can also build upon them. The writing itself remains the paramount factor over which you have control. While strong promotion may increase sales, giveaways and viral campaigns rely on your work's enduring ability to capture the heart and stir the imagination — first, and above all, your own. If you've written a comedy, it should make you laugh out loud. A tragedy? Then the pages of your manuscript should be damp with tears. A romantic thriller? Yes, your breathing should quicken as you reread your manuscript late into the night. The story or book that deeply moves you is more likely, though not guaranteed, to engage your readers.

> **The story or book that deeply moves you is more likely to engage your readers.**

In the end — as well as The End — only loyal readers can make your work into a strong-selling or long-selling phenomenon, and only because they love it. They won't necessarily love it any more just because it won the Booker or the Pulitzer Prize or critics' plaudits. As crime novelist Mickey Spillane wrote, "Those big-shot literary writers could never accept the fact that there are more salted peanuts consumed than caviar."

It's not only "readers" that you must rouse to action but specific groups of readers, usually in the following order: your first readers, your freelance editor, your literary agent, the publishing team, journalists and bloggers, book clubs, the partners and friends of the book club participants, their online and real-world contacts, and so on. You plan on self-publishing? Then just omit the literary agent and publishing team.

If you're dedicated to contracting with an established house but agents and publishers repeatedly reject your work, then you have two choices: you can walk away from your project or return to development. As this book's authors and your fellow writers, *our* objective at this stage is to move you to make the second choice if necessary. We know the value of going back in order to eventually move forward.

> *Our* **objective at this stage is to move you to go back in order to move forward.**

It's never easy to revisit the Develop stage, but it's a choice writers and artists have to make all the time — and at least that transformative third stage should feel more familiar by now. It may help to imagine you're taking a tour of the places where you once lived:

There's that house, the one you passed through too quickly to fully realize its potential. Move back in. Stay as long as you need. Let yourself see it with fresh eyes. Does the master bedroom need dormer windows? Go ahead and install them. Paint the walls blue like you always wanted.

On some deeper level, you knew it could be like this — but maybe you didn't believe it until now. Before long, you'll be ready to throw open the doors and entertain company. But first, savor this time. Before you share, your work's still wonderfully, mutably your own. Make it everything you've dreamed. Indeed, that's the entire point.

YOUR BOOK IN BRIEF

Put it before them briefly so they will read it;
clearly so they will appreciate it;
picturesquely so they will remember it.

— JOSEPH PULITZER

YOU FIRST ENCOUNTERED YOUR BOOK in brief when you drafted a What If question that captured the essence of your project. Now, having reached the Share stage, you need to summarize your story again — this time, for agents, editors, media hosts, and readers.

One question will guide your efforts: *Now that your manuscript is finished, how can you describe the story or central message clearly, powerfully, and briefly?* You'll undertake three important tasks before presenting — or, if necessary, refocusing — your work: itemizing your plot, composing jacket copy, and, if you haven't already done so, committing to a title. As you work on the last two, you experience the five stages in brief — dream, draft, develop, and refine before you share with your first readers, agent, or editor.

If you worked through those exercises described in an

earlier chapter, "Allegiance to Story," and have already created a plot outline, then you may only need to update it to ensure that it covers your latest draft. Alternatively, you should now create a two- to three-page list that captures, in short sentences, what happens in your story, and only what happens, highlighting important turning points. This list of plot points will help you prepare jacket copy that answers your readers' inevitable question, *What's your book about?*

When you draft jacket copy (also referred to as flap or back-cover copy, depending on the book's format), you can draw on your What If question as well as your plot outline. Your final jacket copy should be no longer than one or two short paragraphs, but you may need to distill it down from a longer draft. In contrast to the outline, which covers all major events from beginning to end, your jacket copy comprises only a few dramatic high points, leading toward but not including the book's climax, as an enticing teaser. We pick up books for any number of reasons, but it's strong jacket copy that has the power to glue a book to our hands and open our wallets.

Strong jacket copy has the power to glue a book to our hands and open our wallets.

If you contract with a publisher, then your editor or copywriter will compose the official jacket copy, usually in consultation with you. However, if you draft this copy yourself, in advance, you'll be able to view your manuscript from a new angle — that of a potential reader — and also get a glimpse of what it's like to consciously transition from writing your manuscript to collaborating on the promotion of a book.

Of the exercises covered in this chapter, finding the right

title (and subtitle, if applicable) may prove the most challenging because these few words must speak volumes. Whether you've written a fiction or nonfiction work, your title melds art and commerce. As art, it needs to capture the essence of your work; as advertising copy, it needs to grab your reader. Contrary to the adage, as readers we do and, to some extent, *should* be able to judge a book by its cover and its title. That fleeting first impression can determine a book's destiny.

Contrary to the adage, as readers we do judge a book by its cover and its title.

You'll likely hit on a good title only after you've generated many possibilities. The title may declare itself from the pages of your manuscript. Or in some cases, the story or subject may have itself emerged from a title conceived early on. Since titles cannot be copyrighted, it's not uncommon for different books to pair the same title with different subtitles, though editors prefer not to recycle the title of another book recently published or well known or poorly received. Weak sales are probably not the fault of the title alone, but that's how many editors bet, which underscores the title's importance.

We couldn't use the original title that inspired this book's first draft, because another publisher had already used it for a recently published work. Forced back to the proverbial drawing board, we generated dozens of possibilities, sought more ideas at bookstores and online, looked up synonyms for writing- and story-related words, and free-associated before going to sleep with notebooks close by. Then, as often happens, our perfect title appeared out of nowhere. In general, the author's choice remains a working title and may change if the editor, in consultation with the publisher's marketing department, and sometimes the distributor or book buyers, comes up with an alternate title that they believe will sell better. The publisher has the last word on the title and cover, subject to (in the boiler-plate language of most contracts) "approval by the author, such approval not to be unreasonably withheld."

Once you have a title in mind and have drafted your plot synopsis and jacket copy, it's time to take your draft on a field trip down to the local bookstore. As you walk the aisles, consider:

- ❖ How long do you spend looking at any particular book?
- ❖ What motivates you to pick it up and read the back?
- ❖ What fuels an impulse buy?

When you next feel moved to pick up a book, don't just skim the jacket copy — study it. Compare it with your own, let-ting your eyes roll back and forth between the opening sentence and paragraph of one and the other. Note the transitions and the conclusions. Mentally paste the jacket copy of your book into place and answer the next question honestly: *Would I buy it?* In brief, the answer should be an unqualified yes.

HANDLING REJECTION

Asking a working writer
what he thinks about critics
is like asking a lamppost
how it feels about dogs.

— CHRISTOPHER HAMPTON

NO ONE LIKES REJECTION, but professionals learn to take it in stride and not to take it personally — at least, not to the extent that it alters our behavior from one writing day to the next. As author-poet Tobias Smollett wrote, "Who bravely dares must sometimes risk a fall." Like other artists, we writers like to keep our failures to ourselves. But you can gain valuable perspective and encouragement when you meditate on the collective war wounds of our field's veterans. On rejecting William Golding's *Lord of the Flies*, an editor at Faber called it "an absurd and uninteresting fantasy" — kind words compared to those of an editor who said of John le Carré, after reading *The Spy Who Came in From the Cold*: "He hasn't got any future." Fourteen editors turned down *The Diary of Anne Frank*; they apparently agreed with one editor's conclusion: "The girl doesn't have a...perception, which would lift that book above the 'curiosity' level." On reading Joseph Heller's classic *Catch-22*, one editor wrote, "I haven't the foggiest idea about what the man is trying to say." Another editor dismissed Ursula K. Le Guin's *The Left Hand of Darkness* as "endlessly complicated, and eventually, unreadable." Madeleine L'Engle received twenty-six rejections for *A Wrinkle in Time* before it won over a publisher and the 1963 Newbery Medal committee. And it's well known that numerous publishers rejected J. K. Rowling's first Harry Potter book before Harry found a home.

Numerous editors also rejected early works by authors who would go on to sell millions of books, including but far from limited to George Orwell, John Grisham, Vladimir Nabokov, Irving Stone, D. H. Lawrence, Rudyard Kipling, Frank Herbert, Margaret Mitchell, Norman Mailer, Mary Higgins Clark, Jack London, Pearl Buck, Alex Haley, E. E. Cummings, and Sylvia Plath. Some of them received upward of twenty rejections; others more than a hundred, with Jack London presumably breaking a record by accruing more than six hundred rejection slips before he sold his first magazine story. An editor wrote to tell Pearl Buck, "You don't know how to use English" — she went on to win the Pulitzer Prize for Fiction and a Nobel Prize in Literature.

> Numerous editors rejected early works of authors who would go on to sell millions of books.

The world rejected some authors long before they ever submitted a manuscript: Teachers rebuked a young Leo Tolstoy as "both unable and unwilling to learn" before he left college early. New York University asked Woody Allen to leave, then he flunked out of the City College of New York for good measure. Leon Uris, author of the mega-bestseller *Exodus*, failed high school English three times and never graduated.

All of these writers must have felt discouraged and disheartened after one or more rejections, but they kept on writing. Perhaps they recognized rejection as a multipart initiation into the professional ranks. At the least, they apparently didn't make the connection between rejection and resignation that seems to come naturally to so many of us.

Counterintuitive as it seems, a rebuff may actually benefit us if it leads to our profitably changing course, working on other projects, or self-publishing, because these are beginnings and they usher in new opportunities to succeed that quitting obliterates. As Terry Brooks wrote in *Sometimes the Magic Works*, "A writer can revel in unexpected success, but must learn to live with crushed dreams, as well. If you are a professional, you accept both results with equanimity and move on. Another chance for either lies just down the road." Self-published books may yet attract a large readership and a publishing contract. Another project will build upon the energy exerted in the service of the earlier one.

A rebuff may actually benefit us if it leads to our profitably changing course.

But that doesn't mean you should give up or head in a new direction too quickly in the face of a few rejection letters. While such rejections are a form of feedback, you need to consider their source and take into account the varying and individual tastes of agents and editors. The decision by an agent or editor — or their intern — sometimes says less about the quality of your work than the interests of the reader. It may come down to the subjective nature of art: what one person refuses, another embraces.

An agent, editor, or other gatekeeper may genuinely like your writing but pass on the project because it's not the kind of genre they know or handle. Or, if you write nonfiction, because you don't yet have a big enough *platform* — name recognition, credentials of expertise, track record, or reputation — to help a publisher attract media attention and sell your books. It's undoubtedly frustrating, yet every year many new authors find agents and editors and break through to publication.

In the meantime, if your sense of perspective falls short, your sense of humor may carry you onward. One witty writer, after receiving many near-identical rejections, decided to compose a stock letter of his own. It went something like this:

> Dear Editor,
>
> Thank you for your recent rejection slip, which I found interesting. However, it doesn't fit my present requirements, so I'm returning it. This does not reflect on its merits, so don't be discouraged. I wish you the best of luck in placing your rejection slip elsewhere.
>
> Signed,
>
> An Author
>
> P.S. I apologize for this form letter, but the large number of rejections I receive makes it impossible to answer each one personally.

Of course, you could make the choice to avoid rejection altogether. It's not like anyone's going to force you to submit your work. But what if your favorite authors had felt defeated by early rejections and given up? Let's never forget that it's the professionals' determination to keep on writing, mirrored by their protagonists' unbroken striving, that enables us all to keep on reading.

THE NINE-SALE GAUNTLET

Perfecting and selling your writing is a lifelong task.

— Winston Churchill

To the novice, publishing may seem straightforward: First, find an agent or small publisher. Or self-publish a digital book, then employ a print-on-demand service, work with a publicist, and do some marketing, after which interested readers buy in. But every manuscript's journey has a story arc of its own, and the genre is always suspense. Your manuscript must pass through a gauntlet of nine selling points on the way to becoming a popular book. And at each milestone on the road to publication (and beyond), it can either gain or lose momentum.

With few exceptions, your writing must win over a clique of professional readers who love books and know the market, as much as anyone can claim to know it. In whatever effort you've already invested lies the only influence you will truly have over what happens at each juncture of your book's passage to and through a traditional publishing house on its way to an audience. Note: if you self-publish, only a few of the following sales apply. Let's take a closer look at each sale:

As you can now fully appreciate, you make the *first* sale —
backed by abiding passion for your project — to yourself.

You make a *second* sale to those early readers whose feedback you request. Ideally, their enthusiasm for your story, along
with their candid impressions, helps you take your work to the
next level. If they're sold on your work in progress, that's usually a good sign. If not, let their comments and advice support
your own instincts in guiding revision at the Develop and Refine
stages.

You make the *third* sale to a literary agent or an agency assis-
tant who screens submissions. Search online for a list of literary
agencies and their current submission requirements, then send
the requested materials, usually including a well-composed
query letter, to five or more agencies.

Your query consists of a brief, captivating description of
your manuscript's dramatic core or subject matter, a paragraph
about yourself, and information about whatever platform (marketing reach or fan base) and experience you bring to the table.
Author Nicholas Sparks offers this advice: "Above all, a query
letter is a sales pitch and it is the single most important page an
unpublished writer will ever write. It's the first impression and
will either open the door or close it. Mine took seventeen drafts
and two weeks to write." In closing that letter, offer to send a
proposal or full manuscript on request.

Send out as many query letters as you like, but submit
your proposal or manuscript to only one agency at a time. If
you haven't heard back within two weeks, contact the agency
to ensure receipt and ask when you can expect a response. If
you receive no reply within another week, then feel free to email

or mail your manuscript to another agent who has expressed interest.

If you make that third sale and find an agency to represent you, your agent will provide feedback so you can improve your submission materials, after which they'll forward your work to large corporate publishers or to smaller independent houses. Alternatively, if you don't make the sale to an agency, you can send your query letter to independent publishers, many of which, unlike most larger corporate firms, deal directly with authors. If you come to an arrangement with a small publisher, then you'll probably want to hire a literary attorney or reconnect with literary agents, who are more likely to represent you once you have a solid offer. Literary agents charge no money up front but earn 15 percent of all book-related income. Literary attorneys charge at least one hundred dollars an hour but do not take any percentage of income.

Regarding contracts, bear in mind that you don't get what you deserve in life; you get what you negotiate. And in any negotiation, the power resides with the party most willing to walk away.

Bear in mind that you don't get what you deserve in life; you get what you negotiate.

The *fourth* sale then brings together you or your agent with an acquiring editor at a publishing house. Editors, like college admissions officers, receive many more submissions than they can possibly accept, so they quickly sift out books that they believe won't appeal to either a broad swath of readers or a strong niche. As readers, editors have their own tastes and prefer work that they'd like to take home with them. If they find your manuscript or proposal compelling enough to start and finish reading it, then you've probably made another sale.

For the *fifth* sale to take place, the editor must champion the work's and author's virtues at an in-house acquisitions meeting with other editors and marketing staff. They decide together not only whether they want to publish your book but how much they want it and what they're prepared to offer for it, based on a best guess of first-year sales, factoring in the author's track record and name recognition, if any, as well as the book's and author's perceived marketability and media appeal. If the editor prevails in selling others on your manuscript, then an offer is made and a contract issued. Decisions are made about title and cover that will influence your work's visibility when it's published. This major milestone turns your manuscript into a prospective book. But you're not nearly done.

The *sixth* sale occurs when the editor presents your book to the in-house or distributor's sales reps. During each publishing season, editors oversee a limited number of projects. They may show equal enthusiasm for all of them, but most often, several will take priority as front-runners. The sales force will likely respond to and convey the editor's or marketing director's enthusiasm, and that's important for the next sale.

The *seventh* sale happens when the sales reps from the publisher or distributor pitch your book to online outlets like Amazon.com and the buyers at any remaining book chains. At this point, the chains and independents decide how many copies to order in each store, which makes a significant impact on the initial order numbers. If your book attracts strong interest from media, including bloggers, online newsletters, and websites such as Amazon and Goodreads (now owned by Amazon), the distributor may decide to increase the marketing budget and invest in special online offers and featured bookstore placement or displays that can bump up initial sales, leading to more reorders and fewer returns.

The *eighth* sale connects your book with readers when online booksellers and brick-and-mortar stores, both chain and independent, display and sell your book and when the bulk of your own marketing efforts kick off — an exciting time in the life of any author, whether first timer or seasoned veteran.

The *ninth* and most important sale of all occurs when readers sell the book to other readers, generating word-of-mouth (and "word-of-mouse") testimonials. At its best, such unsolicited, genuine enthusiasm inevitably trumps all advertisements, promotions, and strategies. Unless your book is a huge hit, your publisher can only pump money into special promotions or advertising during a four- to twelve-week window, but the personal recommendations of readers will first boost prepublication orders and initial sales and then keep a book selling over time.

In the end, it's all about trust, and we make it easier by writing a trustworthy and believable book — one that will make early readers exclaim to friends and maybe even to strangers, *"You've got to read this!"*

SELF-PUBLISHING
PROS AND CONS

Whatever you may have heard, self-publishing
is not a shortcut to anything.
Except maybe insanity. Self-publishing,
like every other kind of publishing, is hard work.
You don't wake up one morning good at it.
You have to work for that.

— ZOE WINTERS

BEFORE THE DIGITAL AGE, most writers who self-published did so because they'd failed to find an agent or publisher. This plan B was a less attractive option since the dual roles of author and publisher meant siphoning from one's own wallet to cover the costs of editing, cover art, text design, printing, and promotion, as well as finding a distribution source, which all too often meant storing several thousand books in a garage or spare room and shipping them out one by one.

Self-publishing gurus have for decades offered advice to do-it-yourself authors, who, like single parents, had to do all the work themselves or hire others to do it for them. They assumed all responsibility and risk, often putting themselves in debt on the slender hope that they could make it up in sales.

There were advantages, of course, even before recent advances in technology: Traditional publishers usually take from eight to twelve months to put out a book, whereas a self-published author could have a print book in hand within a month or two. And every physical book sold would net a self-published author about four dollars rather than one dollar per book in the usual royalty arrangement. And if the book garnered respectable sales, the author always had the option of selling the rights to a traditional publisher, having increased the likelihood of doing so. Self-published authors also have decision-making power over cover art, text design, and title. Wresting control from specialists in these fields may not always be the inspired choice, but it does furnish an invaluable learning experience. In the past, however, self-publishing success stories, while real and inspiring, were comparatively rare.

Today's digital and technological breakthroughs have turned the old equations on their side if not quite on their head. Because of diminishing costs and new technologies for printing and distribution, many authors today view self-publishing as a viable option from the beginning. Some veteran authors and industry insiders believe that the issue has reached a tipping point and that the pros of self-publishing may soon outweigh the diminishing cons.

Some veteran authors and industry insiders believe that the pros of self-publishing may soon outweigh the diminishing cons.

You can hire a freelance editor to help clean up and finalize your manuscript. You can self-publish an electronic book in a few days or even hours, making it instantly available, though not highly visible, to a national and international readership. The cost is minimal, ranging from no cost if you use one of the online retailers' conversion software, to a few hundred dollars if you send your manuscript to a professional service that converts your book to a digital format. If you'd like to sell a more traditional print version, you can work through a print-on-demand (POD) service that individually prints and ships each copy you sell. With a modest investment of money and time, the cover art, text, and design of a self-published print or electronic book may look indistinguishable from those of a major publisher. Still, self-published books do have a harder time garnering endorsements from established authors who are less inclined to even consider backing works that have not been vetted by an agent, in-house editor, or publisher.

Regardless, traditional attitudes toward self-publishing are evolving on the heels of technological change. Self-publishing won't have to subsume traditional publishing to earn greater respect. Some traditional publishers now offer self-publication services and have started to publish more authors' works exclusively as electronic books to test the market and reduce their risk. At the least, self-publishing can be a wise entry option (rather than a plan B) for first-time authors who don't yet have a sufficient track record or platform to attract an established publisher. There may come a day when traditional publishers specialize in books that readers have already embraced, and it's hard to dismiss that approach out of hand as a bad thing.

There may come a day when traditional publishers specialize in books that readers have already embraced.

In the meantime, aspiring authors still need guidance as they ask and answer the question, *Should I self-publish?* The answer to this question requires several more:

❖ Do you want to become your own publisher?
❖ Are you prepared to invest the necessary money, time,

attention, and energy in promoting, marketing, and distributing your book?

❖ Do you want absolute decision-making power over editing and design, as well as distribution and marketing?

❖ Will you be able to reserve sufficient time and energy for writing your next book?

No one can answer these questions for you, so consider them carefully in light of your own circumstances. Research current and changing opportunities. Assess your chances of attracting an agent and a traditional publisher — and whether that appeals to you. Seek out opportunities to talk with all the players, both traditional and digital. Don't shortchange yourself merely to avoid rejection. Run your finger lightly down the cutting edge. You can always choose to self-publish after submitting to agents or editors. On or off the page, you're still the decider. Weigh all the particulars with the confidence that every choice eventually leads to wisdom.

MARKETING YOUR BOOK
— AND YOURSELF

To be a successful fiction writer you have to write well,
write a lot...and let 'em know you've written it!
Then rinse and repeat.

— GERARD DE MARIGNY

COMMERCIAL SUCCESS IN WRITING, as in any other field,
requires skill in two arenas: you need to be good at what you do,
and you need to be good at promoting what you do. Your book
can only inform and inspire those who know it exists — and it's
your responsibility to help others get out the word.

Why? Publishers' funds and resources surpass authors',
but the energy that corporate or independent publishing houses
devote to marketing and promotion varies according to their
assessment of each work's potential for success. Larger market realities further dictate that the overwhelming majority of
publisher-driven books receive only a narrow launch window
in which to hook readers before books retreat from front tables
and displays to backlist and back order. Probability, however,
doesn't have to mean destiny — you'll give your book its best
chance for success if you're prepared to champion it no matter
the odds. Many bestselling books likely benefited from marketing

efforts by their authors that matched or exceeded those of their publishers.

So what does the publisher do to promote a book, anyway? The basic aim remains roughly the same: to capture the attention of either a broad readership or a niche audience. Publicity — one facet of the overall marketing effort — means generating excitement about book and author, and alerting potential readers, bloggers, and other media mavens about the project's and your collective virtues. Publicists collaborate with authors to devise a customized strategy based on press kits, video talks, book trailers, or other creative means in order to drive traffic to author pages on publishers' websites and points of sale. Nowadays, both publishers and authors must continuously adapt to evolving media, which rewards innovators who can surf the waves of technological and cultural change and figure out how to turn community into currency.

> You'll give your book its best chance for success if you're prepared to champion it no matter the odds.

Which factor would you guess does more to determine a book's popularity: the quality of the book or the fame and outreach of the author? You'll find industry insiders to argue both sides, but it always comes down to the particular book and author. We can all cite examples of once-unknown authors whose brilliant first novels or memoirs climbed to the top of the bestseller lists, claiming the slot just next to a celebrity cookbook that wafted upward like a soufflé. In most instances, both the writing's appeal and the author's name recognition have important roles to play.

In the months just prior to a book's publication date, the marketing department sets in motion a campaign intended to send a book flying Tarzan-style into the literary marketplace.

Depending on the allotted budget, marketing efforts may include special offers in collaboration with major store and online sellers, email campaigns, select book previews, promotions via social media, and payment for favorable in-store placement as well as greater prominence at online book sites.

Once again, it's vital that you get to know yourself: if you have an outgoing personality, you may readily agree to grant interviews, guest-blog, appear at book signings, organize tele-seminars, reach out to your own network via social media and email lists, and promote your books at speaking engagements large and small. But pace yourself. Even for the most engaged among us, enthusiasm for labor-intensive promotion soon wears thin. There's a saying about authors whose books are adapted into film: the most exciting day in your life is the first day on the movie set, and the most boring day in your life is the second day on the movie set. The same could be said of book signings and media tours.

> **Pace yourself. Even for the most engaged among us, enthusiasm for labor-intensive promotion soon wears thin.**

Many writers dream of going on tour, reading to attentive fans and inscribing special messages in the books they bought, or appearing as a guest on a major radio or television show. Sometimes everything on the road goes according to plan. But on occasion, when you're at your most enthusiastic because it's all so new, only a few readers might show up to your 10 AM book signing on a Tuesday. Or maybe twenty people attend, but nobody buys a book. You've already taken out your pen, so you sit there for a few minutes, feeling a bit exposed but trying to pretend you're just resting. Then, later that afternoon, when you're on air, you realize that the local television host is holding up someone else's book — a heavy-metal memoir, when in fact you've written a sensitive novel about a mother and son in fin de siècle Vienna. And the interview was delayed, so guess who's taking the red-eye to make it to the next morning's local news show? As Dave Barry quipped, "Publishers send authors on long book signing tours aiming to kill the author so their books will be worth more."

More seriously, book tours today, for all but A-list celebrity authors, usually cost publishers more than they directly earn from tour-driven book sales. The same holds true for advertising. That's a major reason why book tours and print ads are giving way to telephone interviews and virtual tours via Skype or Google video and other platforms.

That doesn't mean you shouldn't hit the road. Your marketing efforts for each new book will boost your overall name recognition, credibility, and readership. If you're a new author, you'll want to seize every opportunity you can to draw attention to your subject matter or story. Chance and spontaneity will only bring you so far. Consider developing an informative, uplifting talk around the theme of your book. At first, we recommend you speak at any venue willing to host you — the talk you deliver at a retirement home or school may lay the foundation for a keynote speech at a major convention. Bring books to sell and sign.

What reliably sells books? Good news and bad news: *You* do. Along with your book's story, you'll need to prepare yourself to tell readers who you are and why they should support you — we buy books much like we choose friends. You'll never go wrong by first investing all your energy in producing your best work, but your job's not done until you market that work. In a professional author's life, art leads, but commerce had better quickly follow. Like many things, it comes down to belief:

What reliably sells books? Good news and bad news: *You do.*

when you've written a fine book, don't you owe it to yourself, your publisher, and, most of all, your readers, to do whatever you can to get a book in their hands or to hire someone else who will? It's okay if you prefer to leave promotion to the professionals — just don't forget that you're now one of them.

SIERRA: SHARING ON THE WEB

> Blogs are whatever we make of them.
> Defining "blog" is a fool's errand.
>
> — MICHAEL CONNIFF

WRITING FOR THE WEB makes me think of the time I spent waiting in the wings as a high school actor, my palms damp with anticipation magnified by other bodies standing together in the darkness. I've never lost track of that sense of myself as a groove in the earth through which energy flowed like a river, energy that I could release in nervous laughter and other distracted impulses or choose to channel into my role, sending it outward with each word and gesture. Even if no one else noticed a change, I wanted to feel that with each new performance, I had connected more with my fellow players and the audience.

I make a related choice when I write to publish, at once fully immersing myself in the word-by-word demands of the work and observing my own labors so that I can balance freedom in decision making with the needs of imagined readers. By my late twenties, I'd written for newspapers, magazines, and radio, as well as contributed to several anthologies, but in most cases

I'd felt more like an employee than an author. And wanting to write, for me, always meant wanting to tell stories and explore ideas that felt like my own, in a way that would make my work worth sharing widely. Before the Internet age, earning the title of *author* almost always meant waiting for permission from the gatekeepers. It wasn't that I've ever stopped wanting their approval — and I still write for them — but at some point, waiting started to look less like patience and more like fear. If I had to distill the message I took from the web down to a few words, it would be: stop waiting.

> **Before the Internet age, earning the title of *author* almost always meant waiting for permission from the gatekeepers.**

It wasn't enough to change media, however. I also needed to change my way of working. That meant first stepping back from the crowd and selecting topics that I found fascinating and meaningful, topics that I hoped would inspire greater commitment and vitality in my writing and that might eventually make it more likely that I would connect with an audience of my own. After watching Woody Allen's *Midnight in Paris*, I decided to focus on twentieth-century history and literature because I wanted to write with specificity about a huge, complex, emotional subject. I also wanted to contribute to that small yet significant part of the web that aspires to offer something more than blitzkrieg commentary on what has the most currency.

For that reason, I conceived of a ten-year 20th Century Project, in which I'd spend a full year — in my spare time — reading and writing about each decade of the century. At the least, this project would be challenging enough to mean something if I ever managed to complete it. During the first year, covering the period from 1900 through 1909, I read works by

Rudyard Kipling, Booker T. Washington, W. E. B. Du Bois, Henry James, Anton Chekhov, Arnold Bennett, and Gene Stratton-Porter, among others, supplementing them with author biographies and letters. I wrote long essays, and then I edited them down because the web may be limitless, but individual readers have limited attention spans. The web makes it easier to see that constraints on publishing are human constraints — we often talk as if we're writing for publications, but we're always writing for people.

We often talk as if we're writing for publications, but we're always writing for people.

Publishing, no matter the changes in technology, ultimately describes a relationship between readers and writers and a kind of trust. When I write for the web, I look to that relationship to inspire me to write more, truer, better. I do so because I still believe in that cornerstone of the writing business, on and off the web: that we should be able to distinguish, in terms of its quality, a work that has been *published* from one that has merely been *bound*; that it should mean something to become an author even as that doesn't make it mean any less to be a writer. My priorities change when I write to publish: I fully develop even those pieces that I self-publish online, sticking to my own deadlines yet investing more time and energy in rewriting than a schedule- and paycheck-driven project would justify. And I'm free to do so because it's my own time, my own choice.

I don't know where my own experiments will take me, but I know that they've already changed the way I see the world. And, whether or not the world is watching me, at least I'm no longer waiting in the wings.

DAN: REFLECTIONS
ON THE WRITING LIFE

People are fools to become writers.
Their only compensation is absolute freedom.

— ROALD DAHL

I'LL NEVER FORGET what a photographer friend named Fuji told me soon after a fire destroyed years of his work: "The fruits of my labors are gone," he said. "But the tree remains, and its roots run deep." He clearly grieved the loss, so his words had all the more impact. When I asked him what he meant, he answered with a question: "What if you lost all of the medals and trophies earned over your athletic career — would such a loss erase the value of your training?" As I considered the idea, Fuji added, "The practice of photography enabled me to see in a deeper way. All the images are still inside me, just as your training is a part of you. What truly matters, no one can take away while we live."

Fuji's words have stayed with me because they also apply to any art, especially writing. As poet Cecil Day Lewis once said, "I write not to be understood; I write in order to understand." Not only has the writing life helped me to better understand myself and my world; it has taught me how to handle rejection, how to face self-doubt, and how to push through them both. I've learned to give my best effort on faith and to work toward a specific outcome without relying on it. Over the past thirty years, the writing life has developed my imagination and refined my intuition, opening up those subconscious depths that I believe sustain artists, athletes, and innovators. What others may learn in the military or music conservatory, or on the sports field, or in the seminary — I learned at the computer keyboard.

The writing life has taught me how to handle rejection, how to face self-doubt, and how to push through them both.

The fruits of my work over thirty years remain on bookstore shelves, but it's my mind that holds that intangible treasure-house of memories: in nocturnal solitude and silence, the all-night writing immersion to finish the first draft of a new book, and the deep sense of satisfaction that followed; my first book signing, attended by three people who came in to sit down on a cold evening, and well-attended signings later on; my anxiety during those first television interviews and the learning curve that followed. Most of all, I reflect on the work itself and that purpose-driven absorption as I visited other worlds of ideas and entered stories whose ultimate source remains mysterious.

My own process has changed over the years. Whether I sustain myself with tea and comfort food or prefer to stay hungry; whether I work in the morning, afternoon, evening, or late into the night; whether I jot down ideas with a pen or type them into my phone; whether I aim for a specific amount of minutes, hours, or words — each day, each month, each year, I make new choices that suit the needs and circumstances of the present moment.

My work hours have also changed according to circumstance. During a particularly balanced phase some years ago, I wrote from dawn to noon, leaving time for lunch, then headed off to my day job coaching a college gymnastics team. Many writers aspire to write full-time, but I've found that limited work hours tend to intensify concentration and productivity, not to mention allowing for community to balance the solitude.

Now that I do have entire days in which to write, I find myself carving them up: morning exercise, a short meditation, breakfast, checking email, then working my way into the day's writing. I'll take a break to do some yard work, surf the web, and go for a short walk, before I return to the keyboard. Household chores provide welcome activity breaks.

Gustave Flaubert advised, "Be steady, and well-ordered in your life, so that you may be fierce and original in your work." It's the life I've chosen, the one I've worked hard to achieve and the one I recommend. Having moved from an active to a rather sedentary career, I support my writing with regular exercise; a moderate, balanced diet; and special attention to posture. Spending thousands of hours sitting and tapping at a keyboard helps the writing but can harm the writer. So I take frequent stand-and-stretch breaks and make time for the occasional slow, deep breath, all of which can enhance and extend the quality and longevity of the writing life.

Sometimes I listen to music as I write; other times, I enjoy working in a silence broken only by birdsong or the distant whoosh of traffic. By reading about the lives of different authors whom I admire, I gain additional perspective on the writing life. Over time, I've come to appreciate what does and doesn't work for me.

I keep changing, so I have to keep on making choices, and writing has taught me how. I strive to stay grounded as I stretch, like a tree, to connect earth and heaven. My roots run deep, and the branches are still developing, even now.

EPILOGUE:
YOUR WRITING CAREER

It took me fifteen years to realize
that I had no talent for writing,
but I couldn't give it up
because by that time I was too famous.

— ROBERT BENCHLEY

WRITING HAS NEVER BEEN an all-or-nothing proposition. Most of us sustain our writing and ourselves with the help of a day job, a spouse, or a patron, but for some of us willing to work toward it, a full-time professional writing career can emerge through effort over time.

A handful of well-known writers, including Harper Lee, Ralph Ellison, Boris Pasternak, and Margaret Mitchell, broke through with only one major novel each: *To Kill a Mockingbird*; *Invisible Man*; *Dr. Zhivago*; *Gone With the Wind*. Yet most authors build a career not on one book but on one book after the next, especially since the majority of published works sell only a few thousand copies. Even those whose books sell many thousands of copies experience a rising and then a falling arc. Few of us can live for long on royalties alone.

That's why one literary agent, after congratulating a new author on a book deal, added: "Don't quit your day job." Sage advice, since most published authors need to supplement royalty income with speaking engagements, teaching work, freelance writing, editing, or work in unrelated fields. Many of us continually pitch new book projects, living frugally and writing furiously. Every career will have its peaks and valleys — and that's why we also write to develop courage and stamina.

When asked for guidance, professional authors can only draw on their own life experience. If they do so with an element of chagrin, it's because they can't honestly say that what worked for them will work for you or anyone else. There's no comet's tail by which to ride up to those constellations, no clear trail of stardust left by those who preceded us. You'll need to blaze your own path and, in your own time, discover where it leads. We hope it's clear by now that you make a beginning when you dream.

Blaze your own path and, in your own time, discover where it leads. You make a beginning when you dream.

You can dream of making time to write for its own sake. You can also imagine a writing career. You can entertain the audacious idea of supporting yourself, maybe even a whole family, with words and a little luck. You can envision becoming your own boss, setting your own hours, and pursuing a vocation that enables you to live anywhere you choose. You can put your faith in the possibility that, through a modicum of talent and a continuous surge of hard work, you might one day fill in that blank space on a form under occupation with the word *author*. Sure, the odds are against it, but who ever lived large by trusting the odds? What are the chances of being born on a rare blue-green, water-bearing speck in the universe?

The same dreams that lead to drafts also help you push through passing doubt, one day and one page at a time. And on those days when dreams dissolve altogether — when inspiration, instinct, and experience fall short — you can still move forward through the five stages, within one project or from one project to the next.

If a writing career emerges, it will come from the rotations of this cycle. In any case, you will become, in the words of Henry James, "someone on whom nothing is lost," because every experience will add value to your work and your life.

Author Émile Zola said, "I am here to live out loud." We writers do just that, though none of us lives in exactly the same way. And whether we court celebrity or feel content with the quiet joys of creative anonymity, we share this common bond: writing matters to us. And even as we dream of writing to live, we also live to write.

PARTING REMINDERS

The proverb answers where the sermon fails.

— WILLIAM GILMORE SIMMS

JUST DO IT

If I waited for perfection…I would never write a word.

— MARGARET ATWOOD

If people knew how hard I worked at my art,
they would not consider me a genius.

— MICHELANGELO

The mere habit of writing, of keeping at it, never giving up,
ultimately teaches you how to write.

— GABRIEL FIELDING

I have written a great many stories and I still don't know
how to go about it except to write it and take my chances.

— JOHN STEINBECK

PUT STORY FIRST

That which does not add to a story takes away from it.

— HERB TRIMPE

Children aren't impressed by importance, prizes,
honors — they just want to hear the story.

— ISAAC BASHEVIS SINGER

Stories tell us of what we already knew and forgot,
and remind us of what we haven't yet imagined.

— ANNE L. WATSON

There have been great societies that did not use the wheel,
but there have been no societies that did not tell stories.

— URSULA K. LE GUIN

Feel Your Way

Nobody has ever measured, even poets,
how much the heart can hold.

— ZELDA FITZGERALD

What comes from the heart goes to the heart.

— SAMUEL TAYLOR COLERIDGE

A poet looks at the world as a man looks at a woman.

— WALLACE STEVENS

Listen

First drafts are for learning what your novel or story is about.

— BERNARD MALAMUD

A writer's brain is like a magician's hat. If you're going to get
anything out of it, you have to put something in it first.

— LOUIS L'AMOUR

Three rules for literary success:
Read a lot.
Write a lot.
Read more, write more.

— ROBERT SILVERBERG

Modern writers are the moons of literature;
they shine with reflected light borrowed from the ancients.

— SAMUEL JOHNSON

THINK IT THROUGH

A writer doesn't need an idea for a book; she needs at least forty.

— ELIZABETH PETERS

Humane people who have important things on their mind
almost always write well.

— KURT VONNEGUT

Fantasy, abandoned by reason, produces impossible monsters;
but when fantasy unites with reason, she is the mother of the arts
and the origin of marvels.

— FRANCISCO DE GOYA

Get your facts first, and then you can distort them
as much as you please.

— MARK TWAIN

SPEAK CLEARLY

To write well, express yourself like common people, but think like a wise
man. Or think as wise men do, but speak as the common people do.

— ARISTOTLE

In writing fiction, the more fantastic the tale,
the plainer the prose should be. Don't ask your readers
to admire your words when you want them to believe your story.

— BEN BOVA

The difference between fiction and reality?
Fiction has to make sense.

— TOM CLANCY

LOOK AGAIN

Life is fiction in disguise.

— JAMES MERRILL

A good writer is not a good book critic
any more so than a good drunk is a good bartender.

— JIM BISHOP

No passion in the world is equal to the passion
to alter someone else's draft.

— H. G. WELLS

Creativity is allowing oneself to make mistakes.
Art is knowing which ones to keep.

— SCOTT ADAMS

LET THE STORY CHANGE YOU

A great book should leave you with many experiences,
and slightly exhausted at the end.
You live several lives while reading it.

— WILLIAM STYRON

Writers don't choose their craft;
they need to write in order to face the world.

— ALICE HOFFMAN

You imagine that your pain and your heartbreak
are unprecedented in the history of the world. But then you read.
Books taught me that the things that tormented me most
were the very things that connected me with all the people
who were alive, or who had ever been alive.

— JAMES BALDWIN

COMPLETE THE JOURNEY

All art is knowing when to stop.

— TONI MORRISON

Writing requires devotion and a bit of arrogance.

— BUCHI EMECHETA

Writing is so difficult that I often feel that writers,
having had their hell on earth, will escape all punishment hereafter.

— JESSAMYN WEST

It is not drawn on any map; true places never are.

— HERMAN MELVILLE

Can anything be sadder than work unfinished?
Yes, work never begun.

— HELEN KELLER

Anybody can become a writer; the trick is to stay a writer.

— HARLAN ELLISON

ACKNOWLEDGMENTS

COSMOLOGIST AND AUTHOR Carl Sagan once observed, "If you wish to make an apple pie from scratch, you must first invent the universe." Just so, to properly acknowledge all those who contributed to the making of this or any book, we'd have to stretch back nearly as far, to the early storytellers and scribes, at least, and to Johannes Gutenberg, father of the printing press, up through the inventors of the stylus, the typewriter, the computer, and more. Then come the linguists and teachers and students, the authors and editors and publishers who refined and codified principles of clear expression, and all those who have helped make books available to more readers everywhere. And then come the readers themselves, without whom there'd be no point in writing any of it down.

More directly, we'd like to thank the following people who played a role in this work. First and foremost, Joy Millman — Dan's wife, Sierra's mom — served not only as counselor (and conciliator) but also as our familial editor in chief; she read every single chapter from the roughest draft to the final efforts, offering a discerning first reader's feedback that helped to steer our course.

Linda Kramer of H J Kramer Inc. demonstrated her support and faith in the form of the book contract that officially launched the project. The dedicated team at New World Library, including publisher Marc Allen and, most directly, senior editor Jason Gardner, guided our progress; copyeditor Mark Colucci and managing editor Kristen Cashman helped us choose the right words; Tona Pearce Myers's type design and formatting and Tracy Cunningham's stylish graphic design turned our manuscript into a finished work of art; and Munro Magruder, Monique Muhlenkamp, and Kim Corbin contributed their expertise in marketing and publicity.

We also want to thank our initial manuscript readers, Bud Gardner, Steven Goldsberry, Linda Kramer, Jennifer Martin, Jan Phillips, Suyash Prasad, Erica Ross-Krieger, Ed St. Martin, and Madeline Westbrook, a capable group of people who include an award-winning English teacher, several self-published and traditionally published authors, a creative writing professor, and a member of a university writers group. They kindly devoted their valuable time to reading an early draft and offered their impressions and suggestions, all of which helped shape the content and direction of what became *The Creative Compass*.

Finally, we'd like to acknowledge that it took a village to raise up this book, and we value the opportunity to recognize those names from our own past and present who made meaningful if indirect contributions to this project: China Hoffman, Holly Deme, Alyssa Factor, Hal Kramer, Candice Fuhrman, Michael Larsen and Elizabeth Pomada, Jeremy Tarcher, Janice Gallagher, Rosemary Allen, Ivan Smith, Cochran Thompson, Ernest Contreras, Harold Frey, Michael Pincus, Virginia Forrester, Peter Meyers, Donna Gude, Charlie Wilkins, Jonas Honick, Phil Gutierrez, Jeff Symonds, Susan Clark, Maura Vaughn, David Kudler, Steve Henrickson, Nancy Grimley Carleton, Doug Childers, John L'Heureux, Gordon

Chang, Ted Glasser, Richard Gillam, Steve Stedman, Annissa Hambouz, Allison Zimbalist, Stephen Kinzer, Joe Mathewson, Steve Garnett, Rick Morris, Marda Dunsky, Ruth Hammond, David Wilmsen, Karin Ryding, Rani Kamel, Charlotte Hamaoui, Eleena Sarkissian, Roger Moukarzel, Kaelen Wilson-Goldie, Roseanne Khalaf, Ada Porter, Carole Corm, John Berlinsky, Lea Watkins, Joshua Morgan, Mark Rivera, and Ellen Hardy. Our gratitude to all.

ABOUT THE AUTHORS

DAN MILLMAN, a former world champion gymnast, university coach, and college professor, has written sixteen books read by millions of readers in twenty-nine languages. Dan's work includes fiction and nonfiction, two children's books, and a first-draft screenplay for *Way of the Peaceful Warrior*, released by Universal Pictures in 2007. For three decades he has worked with publishers large and small; represented himself and partnered with top literary agents; toured the United States and overseas; and given hundreds of media interviews for radio, television, print, and online video. A popular international teacher and speaker, Dan delivers keynotes, seminars, and workshops for professional and private clients and associations, and has also taught at numerous writing conferences and retreats.

— www.peacefulwarrior.com —

SIERRA PRASADA is the author of *Creative Lives: Portraits of Lebanese Artists*. While living in Beirut between 2007 and 2011, she reported on Lebanon for radio and magazines and gained proficiency in spoken and written Arabic. Now based in Washington, DC, she works as a freelance journalist, workshop teacher, and editor. Sierra previously contributed curricula to the New York Times Learning Network and earned a master's degree from the Medill School of Journalism in Chicago. Her current undertakings include the ten-year 20th Century Project, a screenplay adaptation, and other fiction and nonfiction projects.

— www.sierraprasada.com —